THE ADHD BOSS
A Promotion and Productivity Handbook for ADHD Employees

Bontle Senne

Dedication

This one is for Samke Zondo (1 March 1985 - 8 September 2012). I hope you made it to the president's office in a different life. I hope one day I will be able to think of you and not sob.

You are the person I think of on all the hardest days. You tell me to pull myself together. You tell me that if you can't, I may as well.

I hope you're proud of me, and I hope I get to see you again, my darling friend.

Contents

Part I
The Big Picture

Chapter 1

The Apprentice: ADHD Edition

When you have Attention Deficit Hyperactivity Disorder (ADHD), people assume you're either going to be a millionaire, an entertainer, a criminal, or homeless. In fairness, many of us are. Having ADHD is the definition of 'no chill' so these extreme stereotypes kind of make sense. We're either working on the project the night before it's due or smashing it out in 30 minutes of random inspiration six months before the deadline.

Finding work that is challenging, flexible, dynamic, and unpredictable is the ADHD holy grail. While we excel in dynamic, fast-paced management roles (Patton, 2009), very few things sound less fun to an ADHDer than the prospect of middle management.

Yet, some of us still want that promotion. Perhaps we believe it will provide us with more opportunities for exciting work; maybe we simply need the money because it buys us freedom; or perhaps we are trying to prove a former teacher wrong about what we can accomplish with our lives. Our reasons are personal and don't actually matter as long as we are clear on them. What matters much more to me is having the resources to make that transition, become an 'ADHD Boss,' and create the kind of workplace I wish I had found at the start of my career.

You cannot coach or mentor your way out of ADHD, but can get better at managing traits that do not serve us. We can become more accepting of ourselves in terms of how our brain works and start working with the tide rather than against it. We can improve at creating inclusive environments where people (regardless of their neurotype) feel the kind of psychological safety necessary to take risks and innovate. We can be bosses who have high-performing teams because we understand that people are far more than resources and we understand the tragedy of not letting people thrive for superficial and performative reasons.

Beyondthat,: we're always looking for a productivity hack or a new system of getting organised that works for longer than three days.

So, naturally, the reason I wanted to write this was because I thought it would be a cool productivity hack to save myself from having the same conversation every week with a different person. Navigating white-collar norms, a culture of masking and rejection sensitivity in the office, are challenges far too familiar to me. As a result, I have mentored dozens of people who have faced the same challenges over the past four years. My advice became a bit of a copy-paste job. An empathetic copy-paste, but a copy-paste nonetheless. Most of the questions were:

- How do I get promoted with ADHD?

- How do I do stuff that bores me?

- How do I manage my emotional stability when office politics get too much, and I feel like I can't take it anymore?

- How do I make people aware of my ADHD without them using it as an excuse to fire me?

- How do I handle overwhelm and overstimulation when my brain still constantly craves stimulation and excitement?

- How do I talk about my ADHD so that people don't think it's a personality trait, a choice, or a cry for attention?

- How do I get promoted if I don't like people enough to want to manage them?

- How do I know for sure if I am ADHD? Maybe I'm imagining it.

Only the last question has an easy answer: almost no one is imaging it. Have you ever thought that you were a teapot? No? Thinking you are imagining your ADHD is a little like wondering if you're a teapot. You wouldn't have even thought of that if there hadn't been a reason for that feeling. I have yet to meet someone who thought they were neurodiverse and turned out not to be. Don't overthink it.

I *have* met many people who think everyone might be ADHD though and they should definitely be thinking a little deeper about what that implies.

While this book has been written primarily for aspiring ADHD managers, I realise that some of the 'we're alllittlebit ADHD' crew are reading this, too. I respect you, but I 100 per cent disagree with that take. I think there is a very big difference between feeling distracted or hyperactive occasionally and being ADHD.

There is plenty of science to support this: The American Psychiatric Association acknowledges ADHD as a medical disorder in its Diagnostic and Statistical Manual of Mental Disorders, which psychologists and psychiatrists use. The DSM-5 (the mental health 'bible') categorises ADHD among neurodevelopmental disorders (APA, 2013). Research supports that ADHD is a legitimate diagnosis recognised by major medical, psychological, and educational organisations, including the National Institutes of Health and the U.S. Department of Education. To point out the even more obvious, ADHDers have increased risks of sleep disorders, psoriasis, epilepsy, obesity, asthma, allergies, diabetes mellitus, hypertension, abnormalities of the eye, immune disorders, and metabolic disorders (World Federation of ADHD, 2021). The general population doesn't have bitbit' of sleep disorders, psoriasis, epilepsy, obesity, asthma... You get the point.

My personal perspective is that neurodiversity isn't even a spectrum. It's a heat map where certain bits light up for one or more people. Describing me as 'high functioning' because I can plan my day out and have a good job doesn't make sense. Context matters. If someone dropped me into a swarming crowd of people, suddenly, I'd become very low functioning. If you put me at the airport when the flight keeps getting delayed by ten minutes every ten minutes, I'll suddenly be very low-functioning. I don't believe it's a scale that improves or declines. We light up some parts, not others.

ADHD As a Heatmap

I try to explain that having ADHD symptoms versus having those traits without ADHD-like is travelling across a continent where you only speak 50% of the languages, but you never know which country you're going to next. The Universe decides your journey.

Sometimes, you are in a country that speaks your home language, and it is easy to navigate transport, accommodation, banking, shopping, and all those other travel things. Other times, you can fake your way through it with some key phrases and copying other people's hand gestures. There are also countries where you don't even recognise the alphabet. It's all just lines and squiggles. Everyone in that country can speak their language. You can't demand they speak your language because it's their home. Lots of ordinary and usually simple activities become quite difficult in that context.

You are the same person in every country, but your context changes. You might always have the same ADHD but they aren't always a problem. Context makes the difference. How we behave and feel in a new country is the ADHD symptom in this example. You're never 'a little' bit yourself in the same way that we're never 'a little bit ADHD.'

The Russian language might equally challenge an English speaker and a French speaker, but the French person may do a bit better in Spain than the English person, given the similarity between those two languages and cultures. That does not mean that the French person stops being French or that they are a little bit Spanish.

In that same way, struggling with some of the same things as ADHD people struggle with does not mean a neurotypical person stops being neurotypical or that they are now a little bit ADHD. I could keep going with this analogy all day, but I think the point has been made.

When I talk to people who say, 'Well, I don't know much about ADHD, and I'm always walking into a room forgetting why I'm there. My partner loses their keys all the time. I think of them as the French person in Spain in my analogy. My answer is always some variation of, 'Okay, but do we lose that same thing four times a day?'

When you walk into a room to find it, do you immediately start to reassemble the radio because we started repairing it last week and left it in pieces on the coffee table? Then do you realise that you need to clean that table now because there's oil on it? So, then do you get up to find something to clean the table, but by the time you get to your pantry, where your cleaning supplies are, you also notice that you are out of juice. If you really need it for breakfast tomorrow morning, do you get in your car and drive off to get juice? Then come home with ice cream? Whatever it was that you went into that room to think about is now a lost, distant memory. Does that happen to you?

Spoiler alert: that does not happen to people who are not ADHD. In many situations, we are the Russian people in Spain. We'd be super competent navigating in our comfort zone, but we may look stupid, lazy, careless, confused or annoyed when we can't speak the language.

I find the attempt to frame general distractibility as equal to ADHD level distractibility problematic because it completely ignores the physiological nature of ADHD symptoms. If everyone gets distracted and it doesn't derail their lives, then ADHD distraction isn't a big deal. That perpetuates the idea that we are 'making it up' on some level.

If this is just something that happens to everyone, then there's nothing to be alarmed by. We don't necessarily need to take medication because everybody else is dealing with it just fine without that medication. But the sources of our traits are not the same as what fuels them in non-ADHDers. So, the way to resolve those is not as easy as 'being more disciplined', 'planning more', 'leaving ahead of time', or 'writing things down on paper'. All of those fantastic ideas. That doesn't mean we can *do* any of that. If we could, we would.

The map below illustrates this idea that ADHD traits just hit different – especially when the situation changes. Look at how the same trait performs across different contexts. Non of these traits are inherently good or bad - it's entirely dependent on where you are and what's expected of you.

Day dreaming is fine when you're alone in a meeting room but brilliant at a music festival. Hyperactivity works great at festivals and Netflix nights but can be challenging in quiet spaces. Sensory overwhelm is manageable alone but catastrophic in stimulating environments. Impatience creates problems in waiting situations but might be fine when you're relaxed. Running late varies wildly depending on what's at stake if you can't be there on time.

ADHD Trait

Context	Day Dreaming	Hyperactive	Sensory Overwhelm	Impatient	Running Late Again
Alone in a meeting room	IT'S OKAY		IT'S OKAY	OH NO!	OH NO!
At a music festival	GOOD VIBES	GOOD VIBES	SYSTEM REBOOT NEEDED — MENTAL SHUTDOWN	IT'S OKAY	
Waiting to board a plane	IT'S OKAY		SYSTEM REBOOT NEEDED — MENTAL SHUTDOWN	OH NO!	SYSTEM REBOOT NEEDED — MENTAL SHUTDOWN
Netflix and chilling	GOOD VIBES	GOOD VIBES		OH NO!	IT'S OKAY

ADHD Traits and Stakes by Context

I think that might be the fourth aspect of why I have a problem with that: saying 'everybody does it', 'everyone's like that' kind of implies that we have the option to be 'less' ADHD, that there is some way for us to turn down the symptoms that do not involve medication. I'm not sure. Well, maybe not medication, but it certainly changes our brain chemistry in some way. That could be through exercise, meditation, or changing our diet. But the point is that we need to change our brain chemistry to do that.

A choice to be different, to start planning more, to think about things differently, is not sufficient, nor is any appeal to religion or religious fortitude, nor is a physiological approach with stoicism saying, 'It is what it is, we have to accept it, ' or some other philosophical content. None of that is going to help us because it's not that we can be less ADHD. We literally can't be less ADHD, and that's super important to keep reminding ourselves.

JOURNAL PROMPTS

> *1. How would you explain the difference between occasional distraction and ADHD to someone who says 'everyone's a little ADHD sometimes'?*
>
> *2. How has your ADHD been misunderstood or trivialised by others? How did that impact you? How does it impact you now?*
>
> *3. What would you want neurotypical people to understand about the 'heat map' nature of your ADHD?*

Our brains function best in response to urgency, excitement, or drama, so we tend to seek out jobs that incorporate these elements. The entertainment industry and the start-up life both meet that brief. Organised crime or emergency medicine could be equally fun. To many of our brains, dopamine is dopamine.

Management and leadership have the potential to meet our dopamine requirements, too. This book takes a broad approach to leadership: it is not about hierarchy. Influence is more important.

That means that an ADHD 'boss' can be:

- A line manager,

- A senior manager of senior managers,

- An executive,

- A person leading from within a team,

- A person leading a group of people.

The contexts I had in mind when writing this book are similarly broad. My experience is primarily in for-profit companies and non-profit organisations, so I naturally have those workplaces in mind. Whether this applies to government or academia, I can't say. I hope that it is relevant. If it isn't, I hope that someone gets inspired to write the 'ADHD Professor' or the 'ADHD Politician.' I would absolutely read those books.

This book is written and structured in a way that no one has to read it from start to finish. Each chapter is self-contained, so you can often dip in and out as needed. You're welcome.

There are four big ideas in the ADHD Boss:
1. **There is no quick fix or hack for your challenges (sorry).** All you can do is find balance between the 3Bs of ADHD: your brain functioning, your internalised limiting beliefs, and your ADHD boss behaviours. Picture them as concentric circles, with your brain at the centre, beliefs forming the middle layer, and behaviours as the outermost ring.

2. There is no standardised method or a generic process for being a boss but systems like my NICER framework can help your chart your own path to success.

3. You don't have to lose yourself in the cult of corporate when there is a Cult of You waiting for you to **step into your power and redefine what success will mean to you.**

4. **ADHD is no superpower**, so your traits are equally likely to be undercover strengths as they are to be challenges. Context is everything.

While Part I of the book sets the scene, Parts II, III, and IV are a deep dive into your brain, beliefs, and behaviours.

This book is a combination of my lived experience, ideas, hot takes, and ideals. I have worked as a journalist, an editor, a McKinsey & Company consultant, the managing director of an education charity, a director at an investment bank, an Artificial Intelligence (AI) founder, and an executive director of a mega-merger. I drank so much of the Kool-Aid in some of my jobs that I am still a little drunk. I have had some disproportionately dramatic experiences in the workplace when I was still trying to shove my whole personality into a consultant-shaped box. This book covers many of these real stories alongside insights from scientists and academics. It is, hopefully, a quick and easy read that leaves you with many questions and tools for approaching your career and competency in healthier, more helpful ways.

I wanted to offer insights you couldn't just Google of ChatGPT and it would be pretty sad if I failed on that one given that I have spent the last 15 years navigating these unpredictable neurospicy waters. I spent most of that time undiagnosed, unmedicated, and unaware of my condition. Today, we're fortunate to live in a time when there's much more visibility for people with ADHD and more information available to help us recognise the signs in ourselves.

One disclaimer upfront though: I don't want you to use this book as a blueprint. Please don't take my journey and my experiences and try to replicate them. There are many reasons for this, but we'll address them soon enough. The short version is that my journey involved many visits to the emergency room, persistent short-term memory loss, the breakdown of a marriage, one psychotic break, and too many 14-hour workdays. Over a decade after my time in top-tier consulting, I still discuss my previous colleagues more often than I do my ex-husband. It is obviously 'therapy speak,' but I really did do the best I could with the tools available to me. If I had known better, I would have done better. I hope this book helps us improve our lives.

I make no judgment, neither positive nor negative, about wanting to be the boss. I think it's perfectly fine to want to grow and get promoted just for the money because none of us are there out of the goodness of our hearts, and regardless of what companies try to convince us, they aren't families. They aren't there for you. They're not our friends. They are places we go to earn money so we can pay for other things in our lives. So, the desire to progress and the willingness to do what we need to, within the boundaries of our value system, do not make us capitalist villains.

The other side is that it is also perfectly fine not to want to be a leader. Not wanting to ascend a performative and sometimes ridiculous management ladder does not mean that we're not ambitious or that we don't take our career seriously enough. It does not mean we're not invested enough in our work or that we will never earn a lot of money. Some of us are just acknowledging that, honestly, some parts of the job suck, and they may not be worth it. For people who work best as individual contributors or those who really enjoy practically doing their technical work, it becomes quite difficult to switch to management because we spend less time doing the thing we love and more time coordinating and coaching people, which just isn't everyone's jam. You'll find no judgment here.

While we're on the topic of disclaimers, I would strongly recommend not modelling your career goals based on mine. My story should not be used as a roadmap for your story. There are two reasons for this: privilege and pain.

Let's set aside the big privileges and start with the ones that seem so middle-class that we forget they are privileges at all. I had the opportunity to study at a top university full-time without worrying about where I would sleep or how I would afford dinner. I had a car when I started work, so I didn't have to wait for taxis or buses to get to the office or home again. I spent many afternoons in board meeting rooms after school, so executives were no big deal to me; it felt more like visiting an older relative. At the start of my career, I was married to a man who cooked, cleaned, took my car in for service, and did the grocery shopping, all while juggling his very demanding corporate job. My ex-husband believed in me. My friends celebrated my achievements much more than I did. I was relatively slim and not unattractive. The common mix of ADHD and childhood trauma often compels me to work for hours or days without breaks. I don't complain about it: I enjoy it.

All of those are privileges that not everyone has. They do not mean that I did not fight for what I have, but they do mean that I had some advantages that successful people rarely acknowledge when discussing how they became successful. If we do not possess these privileges, it is unfair to expect these results from ourselves.

There is a flip side to my kind of privilege, and that is pain.

I do not have children. I didn't have the time or emotional capacity to be a mum and be badass. My emotionally abusive childhood made me unsure that I could be vulnerable or caring enough not to accidentally raise a tough child who turned into a cold adult. My father demanded perfection in every way. There was never any doubt in either of my parents' minds that I would be a boss. I was raised very much for that purpose and to be the sort of person who had a ruthlessly pragmatic view of the world.

The medical condition that makes me work continuously is ADHD. Unfortunately, it also makes me anxious, distracted, overly sensitive, too blunt, easily bored, and unsure of the 'normal' way to interact with or deal with people. Consistently working 12–16-hour days, six days a week, earned me success, but it also gave me digestive problems, back problems, and joint problems. My short-term memory was non-existent. My sleep was a mess for seven years. Despite this, people at work celebrated me as part of our hustle culture, which emphasised constant work. I felt like a failure for not being able to cope without medication. Pain isn't glamorous. I didn't do these things for fun. I thought it was the only way to get ahead.

No one needs to be like me to succeed, so don't try to be. Even in hindsight, I'm not sure what I could have done differently, and I would probably not recommend my career approach to a younger version of myself. There are easier ways to be successful. It will take longer, but we will spend less money on hospital and therapy bills. I know this because I have many friends who have been successful with different choices at different paces.

I share all this at the start of our journey because if you want to be a leader and you have ADHD, it is going to be difficult. There is no way to sugar-coat that and no leadership 'hacks' that last long enough to fuel a career. Some might not want to put in the effort to try because they mistakenly believe that we are ill-suited because of our ADHD, our sensitivity, or our inflexible morality.

None of those things are true, but we don't know what we don't know. That is why it was important for me to write this book not as a hug but more as a shove towards more interesting, radical, and braver things. If we want to be an ADHD leader, a gentle kind of induction may not always be possible. We may not have the option of being nice or having people be nice to us. That doesn't mean that we're going to be evil or unethical, but it's not that practical to be nice when people mistake niceness for weakness. Others may perceive individuals like us as weak for entirely the wrong reasons.

While we can spend our time trying to prove them wrong, I find that somewhat pointless. Actually, very little of the pleasure I experience in the workplace comes from proving other people wrong. I don't care about proving them wrong. I care about having a good life and accomplishing the things I want to do. I care about that for all of us.

We need options. Some people are daydreaming about a corner office with a view. Some need to be reassured that they don't have to be a leader, a manager, or a boss. The costs may be too high for them, and that is totally fine! The lessons in this book are about the ADHD boss mindset, not about our job title. I suggest using this book as a form of apprenticeship.

When I worked in top-tier management consulting, a significant aspect of their training approach was through an apprenticeship model, which differs from the traditional understanding of apprenticeships in other contexts. I think of apprenticeship only as learning by doing and watching others do the same thing. We learn what our slides should look like or how to create a model by observing others teach us. This book is my perspective on being an ADHD leader, presented in my sometimes snarky, sometimes cynical style.

If we approach this book with that openness, we can ignore the stuff we don't need and only implement what is helpful in our context from this literary apprenticeship. Information, like feedback, is a gift. We don't have to like it to use it. We don't have to accept it if we don't want to. We can always give it away if it doesn't fit you. We don't need permission to cut ourselves some slack.

Chapter 2

The 3Bs of ADHD

A DHD is a neurodevelopmental disorder affecting executive functioning in the brain (Carleton & Barling, 2018). Approximately 3.5% of the global workforce is estimated to have ADHD (de Graaf et al., cited in Lauder et al.). The condition affects approximately 2.5% of adults worldwide, according to a meta-analysis of 20 studies conducted across 13 countries (Faraone et al., 2021).

Contrary to popular opinion, ADHD is not a new thing. It has been around much longer than the anti-woke keyboard warriors would like to acknowledge, given that it was first described in medical literature in 1775 by German doctor Melchior Adam Weikard (Faraone et al., 2021). Regardless of the clickbait we have seen, medical experts agree that ADHD is under-identified and undertreated rather than over-diagnosed and over-medicated (Young et al., 2021).

I loved an analogy used in 'ADHD 2.0: New Science and Essential Strategies for Thriving with Distraction' to explain why treatment is so important. If we imagine that our brain is a Ferrari engine and our life ambitions, etc., are a bicycle, the problem is not a lack of power. The problem is not the ability to perform because a Ferrari engine, of course, outperforms everything else, but it's way too powerful for that bicycle. So, the challenge is not so much about increasing our brain's ability to do certain things. In fact, it's about decreasing our brain's ability to overthink and overanalyse (Hallowell and Ratey, 2021).

That makes a lot of sense because when we think about some of the challenges that people with ADHD experience, a lot of them are about excess: over-generosity, over-excitement, feeling overly upset by rejection, an overestimation of the impact of things that are happening to you, things that we will do, and things that we feel are going to happen in the future. So, it makes sense that trying to throttle that back a little bit would be the answer. Medication and non-medication interventions are the brakes, and medication is probably the most effective one.

The stigma about medicating has real costs to people and society: ADHD medication reduces risks such as substance abuse, addiction, smoking, accidental injuries, sexually transmitted infections, and suicide (Faraone et al., 2021). That's important given that ADHDers also have:

- 2x greater risk of alcohol-use disorders.

- 2x greater risk of nicotine-related disorders; and

- 50% higher risk of substance use disorders (Faraone et al., 2021)

These stats make sense. The ADHD brain is always seeking excitement. Drugs are fun in the sense that they stimulate dopamine and adrenaline, making things that otherwise would be incredibly boring suddenly interesting and adding stakes to almost any situation. Do we know what else is fun and exciting? Crime.

A meta-analysis of 37 studies with over 2,300 participants found a small-to-moderate association between ADHD and risky decision-making (Dekkers et al., 2016). We know that many of us find ourselves incarcerated in prison or jail as a result of risky decision-making. Several researchers have found higher rates of criminal behaviour among adults with ADHD (Jackson & Farrugia, 1997; Matza et al., 2005). If prisoners had better access to ADHD support tools, researchers believe there could be a reduction in criminal behaviour of 32% for men and 41% for women (ADHD Foundation). Given that some experts estimate that one-third of inmates in U.S. prisons have ADHD (Arnst, 2003), a 32–41% reduction could make a material difference for thousands of people.

Understanding the Three Levels of Change

If you want things to be different, you need to be different. It's too simple to seem useful. This sounds like the kind of phrase I might expect to see in someone's guest bathroom or at the bottom of a cheerful email signature. Despite being a bit cliché, it is true and deceptively difficult to achieve.

I think of the ADHD brain functioning at three levels, what I call the three Bs:

- The first, innermost level that no one sees is the Brain.

- The next layer is Beliefs.

- The third, outermost layer is Behaviour.

It is easiest to change our behaviour, though it requires repetition, reinforcement, and finding ways to reward ourselves for doing it. Our beliefs are more difficult to change. Shifting beliefs is a more long-term project because they are often limiting, with many layers of mindset, desires, ambitions, and fears underlying them. Embarking on personal archaeology to uncover the bones of our belief system is a long-term project that cannot be accomplished overnight. It is absolutely possible, but it truly requires rewiring what we understand about ourselves in a way that tactical interventions and hacks (which constitute some of our behaviour changes) do not.

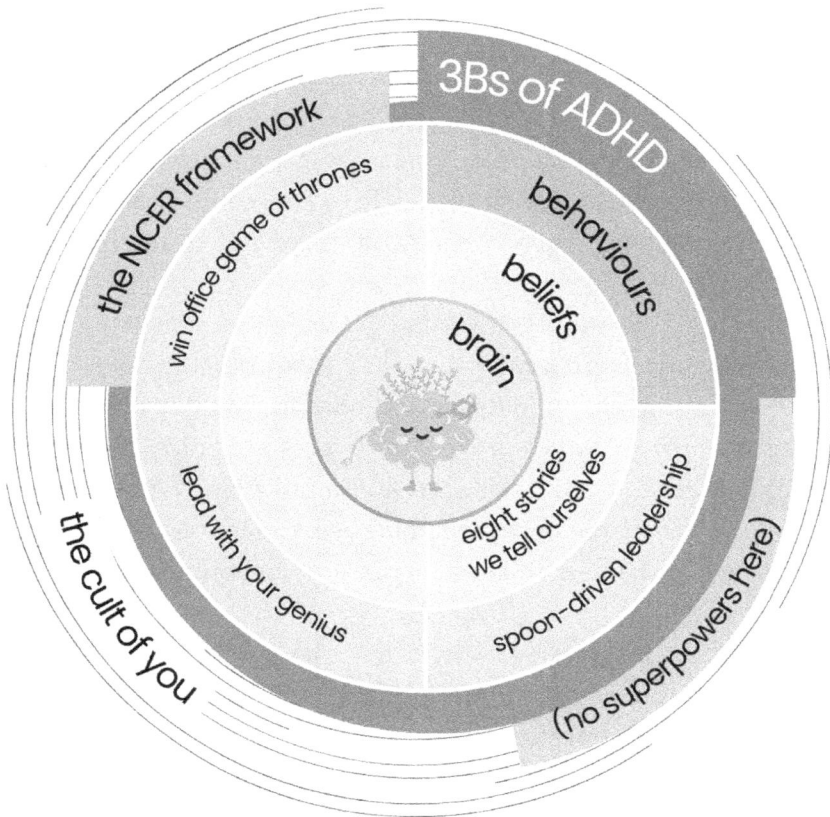

The ADHD Boss Model

Brain: The Biology You Can't Change

At the innermost level of this framework is our brain. The brain encompasses both structure and functioning. It involves both chemicals and synapses. There is cognitive health, knowledge, and expertise, but also mental health and how we interact and cope with others emotionally and socially.

The most important point to remember is that the neurological dif-ferences associated with ADHD are very real. They're not imagined, not merely mental health challenges, and not just personality traits. We can't turn them on or off. Therefore, we're forced to confront the physiological reality of our condition. That doesn't mean we lack aspirations, resilience, or grit, all the qualities needed not only to overcome challenges but also to utilise the unique gifts of the ADHD mind, not merely endure its drawbacks.

Modern research has shown that ADHD involves differences in specific brain chemicals, mainly dopamine and noradrenaline, particularly in the prefrontal cortex, which is like your brain's executive office. Think of dopamine as your brain's reward and motivation chemical. When something important happens, dopamine helps your brain pay attention and focus. In ADHD brains, this system doesn't work quite the same way.

These affected brain regions control three key things: attention (what you focus on), impulsivity (your pause button), and physical activity (how much you move). The prefrontal cortex is packed with dopamine and noradrenaline receptors, and interestingly, children with ADHD often show slightly smaller volume in parts of this region.

One reason for the differences might be how these brain chemicals get recycled too quickly before they can do their job properly – imagine a message being snatched away before the receiver fully reads it. That is an analogy for how ADHD is linked to abnormally low levels of certain neurotransmitters that are meant to act as messages linking parts of the brain. ADHD-associated neurotransmitters are involved in attention, focus, and impulse control (Cleveland Clinic, 2024).

This level is, I believe, almost impossible to intentionally change. We can learn more about ourselves and how to optimise our brain function, enabling it to work more effectively and beneficially. They cannot, how-ever, be fundamentally different.

While it isn't used for diagnosis, brain imaging has revolutionised our understanding of ADHD. Using the alphabet soup of neuroscientific technologies like MRI, SPECT, PET, and functional MRI (which shows the brain in action), researchers can now see differences between ADHD and non-ADHD brains. In one study with over 50 ADHD patients, researchers took images of their brains during rest and while they were concentrating. They found significant differences in several brain regions, including parts of the prefrontal cortex and cerebellum, which help coordinate thoughts as well as movement.

These imaging studies provide compelling evidence that ADHD involves physical brain differences – it's not just a behavioural issue. The research also shows that ADHD brains have different connections between various brain regions. That different networking means that we are wired differently.

Most importantly, these studies consistently find that both adults and children with ADHD show differences in the networks that connect the cerebellum, striatum, and frontal regions – the bits that help us plan, focus, and regulate our actions.

There is plenty of will. The way is the problem. If there were a will and a way, we would find it. That's why we can't just pray or practice our way out of ADHD traits and why seeking treatment is not a sign of failure, laziness, or moral failing.

The way forward probably lies more with accepting our brains than fighting them. We can be a little freer if we accept that it isn't that we won't do something, it's that we can't. If we believe that, it is a little easier to accept that a willingness to change does not necessarily translate to the ability to change our brains.

Your Brain as A Retailer

Stats and numbers do not appeal to or connect with everyone, so I spend a lot of my time thinking about how to explain my brain and behaviour to others. I think of navigating an unmedicated, fully organic, ADHD brain versus an unADHD, or medicated ADHD brain, as the difference between shopping at TK Maxx and shopping at Marks & Spencer (M&S). In Europe, the United Kingdom (UK), and Australia, those references should work. If they don't, replace TK Maxx with TJ Maxx if you're in America, HotMaxx if you're in China, Bokku! Mart if you're in Nigeria, or Dischem if you're South African. M&S is a little more difficult to replace but they're basically like Target, Woolworths, Aeon, Monoprix, or Isetan.

TK Maxx is super fun. The easiest way to explain the store is as a discount clothing, stationery, and homewares retailer with an opportunistic approach. They don't keep loads of stock in any one brand or product. Instead, they source their merchandise from multiple sources: overproduction, discontinued lines, last season's stuff, and competitors who bought too much or just want to clear their current inventory.

I love TK Maxx because you can go every week, and it might have products completely different from what you saw last week. You don't know what brands they have. There is no map that shows you where to find items because the layout changes every week. It's chaotic good with little rhyme or reason for where things are stacked, packed, or displayed. I believe the company itself refers to shopping at TK Maxx as a 'treasure hunt' experience. That level of unpredictability is fun but it's not efficient. That's why the unmedicated brain is basically a branch of TK Maxx.

You can't go to TK Maxx and say, 'I want a red polo shirt, size 10.' You just go and check what happens to be there that day. In the same way, finding specific information or memories is difficult for the ADHD brain to do on demand. That's how I often forget very important information about myself like the fact that I don't like eggs. Sometimes I go so far as buying and cooking the eggs before I realise that I hate eggs.

In contrast, at M&S the aisles are the aisles. They're always the same and the products across all stores are roughly the same. They sell clothes, homeware, and food with a value proposition of quality and value. If you go into an M&S food store, this section will be for the fruit, then it's going to be vegetables, then all of these fridges, then canned foods, then cleaning supplies with alcohol usually in the furthest aisle from the back. Going into a store is always the same, and the product you're going to get is predictable. The unADHD or medicated brain is an M&S.

There is no objective benefit to going to TK Maxx and M&S. On different days, with different budgets, and different moods, we may prefer one over the other but it's all just preference.

In our natural state, for better or worse, our brains are more like TK Maxx than M&S.

This is why we sometimes don't have consistent access to information about ourselves. I went through two weeks of walking into the grocery store to buy food to cook and not being able to remember what food I like. I ate a lot of apples, oranges, and bananas that fortnight. It only stopped when my friend send me a photo of a beautiful vegan salad she had made. Suddenly, I remembered chickpeas, avocado, peppers, and a bunch of other ingredients that I regularly cook with.

That is not going to make sense to many neurotypicals but it happens. The TK Maxx vs M&S analogy at least explains what is happening if we keep making the same mistake over and over again, even when we should know better.

Beliefs: The Psychology You Can 100% Change

People tend to think our beliefs are fixed, like our brain structure, but beliefs are things that can be shifted, albeit with significant effort. We no longer have to continue believing the same things about ourselves, the world, or the workforce.

All that negative self-talk that we go through is a question of trying to think through what our script about leadership is. What are the things that we believe about leadership and leaders? Perhaps we believe we are not very good at it. Perhaps we believe we are excellent at managing people, but we have no evidence to support that claim. Perhaps we think that others have tried to sabotage our leadership in the past.

Perhaps we believe that our leadership must adhere to a specific model, and we are unsure whether our authentic approach is sufficient or effective enough. Perhaps we think that this is a service or a duty we are performing for our team in leadership, and it is something that will attract a lot of criticism and judgment from them, which might make us feel nervous about it. The point I am making is that there is always a story we tell ourselves, which may or may not be grounded in reality. However, perception is our reality, and it is the thing that ends up being the handbrake on our ability to start and keep going. The one thing I want to encourage after filling out the leader's script template is to ask, 'Is it true? '

When we really interrogate these limiting beliefs and really start to think about whether they are real, whether they are grounded in something, whether they are just a response to past hurts or triggers or trauma or just the way that our brains are trying to keep us safe from future challenges, when we ask the question, is it true, that opens up the possibility that it might not be. And if it is not true, then that might be something we need to rework and reconsider.

Behaviour: The Most Realistic Starting Point for Change

ADHD symptoms tend to decline with increasing age, with greater decline seen for hyperactive-impulsive symptoms but less so for inattentive symptoms. Adults with ADHD can, therefore, have a more subtle presentation characterised by more internalised symptoms rather than overt externalised behaviour. This makes it more difficult for ADHDers to 'prove' that they are struggling but should have no impact on how successfully they can change those external behaviours and manage those internal symptoms.

Behaviour is thus the easiest level of the 3Bs to shift because we don't actually have to change our beliefs to change our behaviour. Sometimes I think that changing our behaviour creates habits that then become the foundation for new beliefs. This is the principle I have applied in this book: first, try to do the thing, then try to understand it, and only then can you change how you think about it.

This approach works particularly well for ADHD people because we are not particularly good at having full access to all information about ourselves at all times. There is real variability in what I know and feel about myself day-to-day. For example, I know I should never book a red-eye flight or schedule anything at 6 am because I'll inevitably miss it. I'll remember that for months, then one day think, 'Wouldn't it be great to save money and catch a 5:00 AM flight?' and completely forget why it's a terrible idea for me.

For many of us, we don't always know what we are feeling in the moment or what we think about something. We may be unclear about the origin of our beliefs unless we have undertaken a significant amount of personal excavation, as I mentioned.

It is simpler and more pragmatic to start with behaviour and use how we feel about those behavioural changes as input to help us understand our beliefs better. This will help us uncover some of our limiting beliefs.

This is a little different from 'fake it 'til you make it' and much closer to 'your thoughts become your reality.'

ADHD Behaviours in the Workplace

Many successful ADHD managers thrive in fast-paced, hectic roles due to their quick decision-making and adaptability (Arnst, Carroll & Ponteretto, cited in Patton, 2009). That may be why ADHDers often choose alternative career paths and perform well in dynamic environments like sales or tech, where they can be creative, independent thinkers (Robbins, 2017). Those who default to or choose more mainstream, stable paths do not always do so well.

After secondary school, despite high levels of intelligence, it is estimated that only 5% of ADHDers complete college or university (Patton, 2009). A Scottish study of over 750,000 students provides some insights into why that might be. ADHD students were:

- 3x more likely to have low educational achievement.

- 2x more likely to drop out before age 16.

- 8x more likely to need special education; and

- 40% more likely to be unemployed (Fleming et al., cited in Faraone et al., 2021)

When we think about what ADHD means, many of us still have that troublemaker child who won't shut up in class in mind. Adults have ADHD, too, but symptoms decline with age—less hyperactive-impulsive behaviour and fewer inattentive symptoms. This is great for obvious reasons, but terrible because fewer symptoms lead to a more subtle adult presentation. It makes it more difficult for ADHDers to 'prove' that they are struggling and have ADHD (Willcutt, cited in Young et al., 2021).

If no one believes us, we're not getting access to any of the support we need. If we don't get the support we need, it is difficult to succeed as adults with ADHD.

ADHD employees are more successful in workplaces where colleagues and supervisors understand their challenges and support their strengths (Garber, 2001; Robbins, 2017). ADHD symptoms that typically cause challenges to promotion include poor time management, missed deadlines, and organisational challenges like cluttered desks and misplaced paperwork (Nadeau, 2005).

We know that ADHDers who are able to develop coping strategies, particularly for impulsivity and attention regulation, are 20% more likely to reach senior leadership positions than those who aren't.

ADHD employees typically earn between $4,334 and $10,791 less annually than their non-ADHD peers, amounting to approximately $77 billion in lost wages annually in the United States (Robbins, 2017). In case that wasn't depressing enough, ADHD workers lose an average of 22 days of role performance per year compared to non-ADHD colleagues (Faraone et al., 2021).

Over 75% of people report that their ADHD symptoms negatively impact workplace relationships with their majority neurotypical colleagues (Hotte-Meunier et al., 2024). There is a range of very normal ND symptoms that become 'issues' in the workplace, including:

- Difficulty noticing social cues.

- Tendency to interrupt.

- Excessive talking.

- Being perceived as blunt or straightforward, and

- Risk of being viewed as 'troublemakers' or 'uncaring' by colleagues (Hotte-Meunier et al., 2024)

While ADHD employees can be coached and mentored like everyone else, their fundamental ADHD cannot be 'developed away'. Asking someone to suppress their natural tendencies or traits places an unsustainable cognitive load on them, leaving less energy for meaningful work.

TRY THIS: An ADHD Traits Inventory

Make a list of your ADHD traits, dividing them into three columns:

- *Things that feel like superpowers*

- *Things that are context-dependent (i.e., helpful in some situations, challenging in others)*

- *Things that consistently create friction*

Look for patterns: Which traits show up most at work? Which ones get positive feedback? Which of these gives you advantages or challenges in situations where you are taking a role leading others? Could you use any of your strengths to counteract or mitigate your challenges?

Our Brain and Beliefs Don't Need to Be Our Enemies

When it comes to our brains, we need to work with them rather than trying to change them. There is no point in trying to make our brains different; the sooner we accept that, the sooner we are free to move on and change our beliefs and behaviours.

Let me share a personal example. Like many people with ADHD, I suffer from a form of task paralysis when I have an appointment in the afternoon, but nothing specific to do for the rest of the day.

When I say, 'nothing to do,' that is a bit of a stretch because I could work out, clean the house, walk my dog, clean my car, do some work, or read a book. There are multiple activities I could theoretically engage in, but the appointment looms large in my mind as something immovable that dominates the rest of the day. As a result, I am unable to do almost anything for the entire morning. I might end up daydreaming out the window for hours before that appointment.

Interestingly, afterwards, I became incredibly efficient because that activity somehow unlocked the paralysis. This mix of both overwhelm and underwhelm results in nothing productive happening. When these two states cancel each other out, it is not an efficient use of my time, and I am absolutely aware of that. However, I also cannot help but notice that my brain does this.

There is nothing I can do to change this aspect of my brain. I can, however, do things like schedule my meetings for the first thing in the morning so that I don't have to wait too long, and my brain does not unnecessarily waste time being paralysed when it could be solving problems or figuring out how to get more enjoyment out of life.

This is why I almost never attend afternoon meetings unless I have already had morning meetings. Otherwise, it creates this weird situation where I waste hours. This example shows changing my behaviour because I believe that task paralysis is not the most beneficial use of my time, and it does not align with the mindset and version of myself that I am trying to build.

Taking a social model of disability and thinking about task paralysis not as something wrong with us but rather as something that happens as a result of demands made on us externally, makes us realise that we are quite able to change our situation. We can change the beliefs we might have about it, even if we cannot change the fundamental fact that our brains will continue to exhibit that behaviour every single time, regardless of whether we would like them to or not.

Remember this as we move forward: work with our brains, change our behaviour, and over time, our beliefs will follow. This is the path to becoming the leaders we want to be with the ADHD brains we already have.

Part II
Making Friends with your ADHD Brain

Chapter 3

Invisible Struggles

Calm Through Crisis: Comfort in the Uncomfortable

I think the other challenge I experience is being the calmest, happiest, and most cheerful in an emergency or distressing situation. Often, barring an experience with sexual assault or harassment, if something is going wrong, there's a big deal that may or may not close tomorrow, my car tyre has blown out, a number of these things. If I'm not in a life-or-death kind of situation, anything lower than that is something which actually makes me pretty cheerful.

I'll be having a super bad day because nothing's going on, then someone smells fire in the building, and everyone has to evacuate. I'm suddenly the person cracking jokes and having the time of my life because non-fatal emergencies are fun, right? Those extreme situations are a good time. That's kind of how people with ADHD end up with addictions of all sorts, getting into crime of all varieties, because those things are consistently fun. They're unpredictable by their nature; we love the unpredictable. We live in a space of irrationality; we really enjoy things where the content is uncertain and ambiguous. It means it can change. It means that we can change it; we kind of love that.

The other side of that is that I am frequently setting my life on fire. It feels like I'm doing it just to watch it burn because there's no other reason. I feel like I'm reinventing myself at least twice a year with a different career, a different aspiration, a different look, a different serious hobby, or obsession. On some level, this makes me a pretty interesting person to have as a friend. But on another level, I am sort of tired of everything becoming a story, everything becoming some sort of anecdote that I can share with others.

It is really difficult as an adult to have that kind of excitement on a regular basis because routine is what builds psychological safety. Consistency is what builds psychological safety. So, we may never really feel safe about opening ourselves up to people about sharing what's going on with us because everything is always changing, including you. That makes it super hard to ask for help.

We don't want to be perceived as weak. We don't want to be perceived as not being able to get stuff done.

Masking: Do Not Bring Our Full Self to Work

Before we dive in, let's talk about something fundamental: masking. The concept of masking is pretending to be neurotypical to escape judgment and rejection that might follow from behaving naturally. For example, if we are a young girl in the classroom and see how teachers respond to boys causing disruption, running around, or not sitting still, there is judgment and attempts to discipline the child. Sometimes, we get great teachers who manage this well, and sometimes, we get teachers who, while competent and wanting the best for their students, do not have the right training or understanding.

Girls watching this behaviour may understand they feel the same impulsivity, restlessness, and wildness as that boy, but they learn that showing it gets them into trouble. They start to mask by looking at what others who are not getting into trouble are doing and mimicking that.

This mimicry becomes so persistent that it is like a mask we wear. We are not even sure what our real opinions, beliefs, or reactions would be because we have spent so long trying to make sure they match what a group, community, organisation, or friendship group might expect.

Research tells us that the vast majority of ADHDers in the UK are scared and reluctant to disclose their diagnosis at work due to fear of negative impact on their careers (Norman, 2023). The is not unreasonable. ADHD disclosure has long been represented 'career-limiting move' because of how organisations have responded in the past. That is why even progressive companies that aren't looking to put all their ADHDers on performance improvement plans find it difficult to identify and prevent the type of masking that contributes to ADHD employee burnout.

Organisations can offer education about masking, but people will only stop masking when they feel safe enough to. In the meantime, our employers can also offer access to well-being, wellness, and health support for when their people burn out, whether ADHD or not.

There is also an argument that all employees mask to some extent. None of us would say we are always our full, true, and authentic selves in the workplace. Sometimes, our true authentic self might be someone who wants to play World of Warcraft for 20 hours a day, but we understand that it is not possible in a work environment if we have a mortgage to pay. We have to pretend to be the kind of person who has other deep and meaningful interests, one of which is, hopefully, our job.

Whether we actually feel that way is somewhat irrelevant in the workplace. We want people to be their authentic selves, but only within a safe and specific context. Thinking about masking as something only neurodivergent people do is one of the mistakes employers make and a wasted opportunity to provide safe spaces for people who want to unmask, regardless of their neurotype.

Overwork: We Can Burnout from Too Much or Too Little Work

Standard KPIs that measure employee input versus output might not always make sense for all ADHDers. Studies show that ADHD employees report higher levels of job burnout compared to their neurotypical counterparts (Turjeman-Levi, Itzchakov & Engel-Yeger, 2024).

I've experienced burnout. I have also been in situations where I handled two or three roles at once without issue, but I struggled when my workload decreased.

The period in my life when I felt most intellectually fulfilled was a continuous loop of over. I worked for a large telecommunications company. I was the people director for the commercial team, responsible for around 7,000 employees' HR in the company's largest department. Alongside this, I managed the small HR operations team and all the business partners for the entire organisation. Obviously, that was not enough, so I also retained my original role overseeing transformation, governance, and value assurance across major projects. Because my sharky boss realised that that wasn't enough, I then started doing strategy and M&A work. This workload finally gave my brain the stimulation it craved. right up to the edge of overstimulation.

Others might have felt entirely different about that kind of workload. It's certainly not a sustainable approach for everyone, but for someone with ADHD, having more work can actually be beneficial rather than overwhelming.

Even acknowledging that burnout might be more likely when we have less work, 100% utilisation is not a good idea.

I get it. Being busy every hour of the day may seem like a dream for people who often waste time being distracted and not getting things done. It might seem particularly beneficial, advantageous, and quite sexy to feel like we are living our best life by being super productive at all times and living each day like it's our last. However, in that situation, we don't have time to deal with emergencies or things that come up last minute. We don't have time to reflect, to think, and to give ourselves the space and silence for some of those more creative, abstract connections to be made.

We need to give ourselves plenty of time for learning because learning is not always as linear as we think it is. Sometimes, it requires curiosity to go down potential dead ends, not seeing that as a waste of time but rather seeing it as information we are gathering for future synthesis. The whole Steve Jobs thing about not being able to connect the dots going forward is completely right. If we don't create that space, we don't get to put the dots down for us to figure them out going backwards, either.

This inconsistency is what I mean by 'not always having reliable sources of information about ourselves.' We can forget what's good or bad for us, even after learning those lessons repeatedly. It takes years of reinforcement for these lessons to stick because they're often counterintuitive. They go against what our brain craves, usually excitement and stimulation, not necessarily what's best for you. For instance, excitement is often tied to crisis, instability, or chaos. I often perform better under such conditions. I remember one day when I was upset about discussing the closure of our department with my team. Suddenly, the fire alarm went off. At first, I thought it was a drill, like everyone else, until the fire officer announced, 'This is not a drill. ' Smoke began to fill the air, and instead of panicking, I felt strangely upbeat. The crisis provided a huge dopamine hit; my ADHD brain thrived on the urgency and energy of that moment without even considering the dangers.

This is one of the challenges with our brains: sometimes, they don't signal fear or danger when they should, and similarly, they don't signal when certain behaviours are inappropriate in a work context. This means that ADHD people might make the same mistakes multiple times, even though I've always believed that receiving the same feedback twice indicates we're not learning fast enough. Unfortunately, sometimes, that repetition is unavoidable. So, it's crucial to have a leader who can manage the inevitable fallout from repeated mistakes.

Object Permanence: If I Don't See It, It Doesn't Exist

One trait that really impacts my day-to-day life is my lack of object permanence. We know that thing where if we hide our face behind our hands like a baby and then remove our hands, the baby starts laughing. For the baby, we ceased to exist the minute we went behind our hands or went behind the door or whatever it was, because they don't have a sense of object permanence.

But for me, I'm kind of like a baby – if I don't see it, it doesn't exist. So that means that food can go rotten in my fridge and stay there for ages because I just didn't notice it was there. I often forget to eat things that I might be super excited about. Having tools like WhatsApp, Slack, or whatever has been incredibly helpful for me to keep in touch with family and friends, not just because it's easy to communicate that way, but actually, because there's a list of contacts. Every time we go into a message someone, we can see our other contacts, like, 'Oh yeah, I haven't messaged my mum in a while'.

That even happens to me with people with whom I'm in a romantic relationship, if I don't see them, the feelings that I have for them are much reduced. To be honest, it's almost like they don't exist. That isn't very comforting to people because I'm not making that a function of time. It doesn't mean that because I haven't seen you in two weeks, it could be two hours that I haven't seen you, but I might forget that we are in a relationship. That's, unfortunately, just the problem of object permanence.

Executive Functioning: ADHD Doesn't Have a More Efficient 'Work Mode'

There are a couple of traits that any ADHDers in the workplace should know about. One is going to be around problems with organising and planning things, especially in the long term, this is mostly for our tasks and those of our team. It's called executive function, which is roughly an umbrella term. People with ADHD are not great at thinking through the longer-term consequences of what they're doing at the moment.

This also means that we have a real wandering mind and constantly changing interests. That can be really difficult for people to understand because we appear to be a little bit dreamy, a little bit in our own space, not paying attention, or being unreliable. But the problem is that we're paying attention to too many different things at the same time. Our brain is going several hundred miles a minute, lying in bed at the end of the day, our mind isn't wandering; it is racing, making it really difficult to turn that off.

There is a tendency to procrastinate and then burn out through working to excess. Working to excess often results in short bursts. So, when I had to write my master's thesis, for example, I had nine months to do it. I did it in two and a half months because I couldn't start writing it until two and a half months before it was due. That was very concerning, obviously, for my supervisor, whom I had not communicated with, because I genuinely forgot that he existed, because he hadn't emailed me or called me or whatever.

Once I did start, I got it done in two and a half months, which was great; however, it involved so many all-nighters, overworking, and skipping my actual day job so that I could work on my dissertation. That kind of intense, manic-like work, while it is effective at getting things done, is not an efficient way to work. It's certainly not a sustainable way to work. But for some reason, we ADHD folk frequently find ourselves in situations where a task that should have taken two weeks takes two hours, but we are only doing it on the day that it's due. That lack of forward planning can be really difficult.

There is something about our inability to sustain any level of boredom, which I think is also important. It means that we really have this impulsive, impatient nature that wants to get results now, that wants to do things now. It is a shoot-first, ask-questions-maybe-never kind of approach to life. That is unfortunate in a lot of situations as a leader because we do want to give people the time, especially to think through ideas, to be able to be adequate thought partners and give thoughtful responses. I physically have to hold myself back from just solving problems for them because it would be faster for me to do it, and I don't have the attention span to deal with trying to wait for them.

Chapter 4

Invisible Strengths

Intuition and Uncommon Sense: Knowing What Advice to Ignore

Some of the most fundamental training we receive about obtaining and maintaining management positions may not make sense for people with ADHD. This isn't because the training is irrelevant to them or because they're so amazing that they've already mastered these topics. Rather, applying these principles implies some element of choice, the ability to choose to behave in certain ways. While people with ADHD can create guardrails and systems to prevent behaviours they fundamentally don't want to exhibit, there is nothing they can do to make themselves less distractible. They can take medication, but they're not fixing that behaviour. They're just lessening it for specific periods.

Even when we consider executive functions, success isn't necessarily tied to how good those functions are. I don't miss appointments, I don't let people down, but that has everything to do with the kind of work I do and the people I work with, who are happy to fill in some of those gaps. It also has to do with having the right support system. That means alarms just go off, food is delivered, and people show up to do whatever needs doing, so I don't actually have to think about it. I'm not consciously making any of those choices; they're just systems I've set up to work in particular ways.

Some of the advice, though, is actually infinitely sensible. I'm going to discuss both sides of it, starting with the advice that isn't great, simply so we can end on something more positive and actionable. ADHD people are nothing if not eternal optimists.

Begin with the End in Mind?

One of the most common pieces of advice is 'begin with the end in mind', which I know is one of the seven habits of highly effective people. Sometimes, it's discussed as 'plan in advance, stick to the plan' or 'failing to plan is planning to fail.' This is a good suggestion because creating and following long-term plans (having three-year, five-year, and ten-year plans) is actually beneficial. We know that setting these goals and writing them down improves the likelihood of achieving them, if we believe some of the pop psychology from business schools over the years.

However, the concept of detailed long-term planning probably won't work for people with ADHD for several reasons. First, the future is so abstract that it may be difficult for someone to visualise the path from where they are now to that distant point. It may, in fact, be such a distance that they don't really feel capable of planning that far in advance, understanding what they do about their limitations. This can happen to anyone, but there's also something about the detail and attention required for rigorous, long-term planning that poses particular challenges.

We are often excellent at seeing the big picture, but paying attention to details requires a narrowing of focus that we're typically not good at. It's difficult for us to forgo the flexibility of being more agile and able to change things as we go along. Suppose we believe in agile ways of working in general. In that case, we understand that creating a comprehensive plan at the outset of a long-term activity or goal may not always be necessary, as we often lack complete information upfront. As time passes, we work on something, and through feedback, testing, learning, and building, we become much clearer about our vision.

It's not a bad thing to acknowledge that all future planning is, in some sense, imaginary. It makes more sense to do iterative planning where we have a broad objective or goal in mind, but can adjust, adapt, and change as new information emerges and contexts shift. Being able to abandon the plan when it's no longer working is something every leader could benefit from. There comes a point when trying to stick to old ways of working, or even an idea that seemed fantastic at the beginning, no longer makes sense. Admitting we are wrong is something people generally find difficult, but the leaders I've respected most are those who've been authentic and honest enough to admit their own failings. I know that both authenticity and the ability to be brutally honest, even about us, are certainly something someone with ADHD is capable of doing.

Find Work-Life Balance?

Being able to separate one's personal and professional lives and maintain a work-life balance is really hard. I think for someone with ADHD, we get so enthusiastic and excited about new ideas and creating things, which spills over into our work. As much as we would like to work to live instead of living to work, the reality is that sometimes work feels like play for us. This makes sense, given the way kids are socialised and rewarded for academic excellence, and as adults, we're rewarded for excellence in our labour. A person can become addicted to the dopamine associated with that sense of reward.

When ADHDers adopt a different mask for their personal and professional life, it may be an additional cognitive burden. For that person, it amounts to having to play three roles: we in private, we in public, and we when we're alone, which I think is honestly too much to ask of anyone.

I think I was really lucky that my obsessions, the things that really interested me and elicited hyperfocus, happened to be the things I was working on. As a result, it became even more challenging to separate my personal and professional interests, as I was genuinely passionate about those topics. It doesn't mean it's not still a job; it doesn't mean I would be doing it for free, but it certainly did mean that a lot of what I wanted to talk about was my work, not because I thought it was so important, but because it genuinely was something that was taking up a lot of my mind space.

There is this tendency we have as people with ADHD to have really intense bursts of work, which can very easily lead to burnout. It would be much easier to spread our energy and efforts over time more consistently, but that often isn't how it works out because we tend to procrastinate since we're not super good at understanding how long something will take. It means that while other people will benefit more from a 50-50 split between work and life, we may benefit from a 10-90 split. For people like me, I actually thrive very well on a 70-30 work-personal life split, just because so much of my work is what I'd be doing for leisure a lot of the time.

For example, writing and reading become things that I do for work. Sometimes, I just get so interested in a topic, like I did about women's experiences in relationships and dating, that I decide to write a book about it. So, if I'm reading about that, if I'm writing about that, is my hobby now a personal topic? Is it now professional because there's the possibility, I could get paid for it? When I discuss it, is it inappropriate to bore my friends and family with this topic, considering it's my job? I also don't necessarily want to talk about my sex life with my work colleagues. Therefore, it becomes extremely challenging to establish a clear demarcation. I think trying to tie ourselves in knots and trying to create one doesn't necessarily make sense. It might be easier to accept that there may not be a clear distinction between these two things for us as long as we manage our energy appropriately and maintain the systems we need for good health. That's the most important thing.

Respect The 'This Is How We Do Things Here' Mindset?

People with ADHD are not really good at following processes. We're not great at following established rules or protocols for behaviour. We're not good at people saying, 'Be more professional, ' which often means we're not good at following traditional career paths. It's a challenge for us to stick to those norms, not because we don't want to, but because we are, in some sense, kind of incapable of doing it. I really loved how, in 'ADHD 2.0', the authors talk about how we're not trying to go against the status quo—we just didn't know there was a status quo we were going against (Hallowell and Ratey, 2021).

I think it makes sense a lot of times to follow procedures in situations where there is a high risk associated with not doing something in a particular way. By 'risk,' I mean something that's really consequential, not like in our heads. For example, starting a pilot coaching support group during lunch breaks might feel risky because people may not want to do so or because it requires some emotional vulnerability, but it's not actually a risk. The actual consequence is very low compared to the consequence of pressing a button in a nuclear facility.

Understanding the difference between rules that matter and rules that don't matter is really important for leaders because sometimes we can swing too far on that pendulum and decide that none of the rules matter and none of the norms matter—that professionalism is a thing people made up to keep people in a system that benefits from their labour. It's not entirely untrue, but it's also not something we want to stick to as a hard-and-fast rule. The point of our brains is that we can be flexible and adapt. We should take that as an invitation to occasionally adapt to the rules and established protocols because it makes sense to do so, because there's an important reason to do so, and there are real consequences to not doing so. Going against the grain just because that's our first instinct is not necessarily always the right instinct. People who want to stick to those lines aren't necessarily wrong for doing that.

I think it's also important here to draw parallels to others - ND and NT - who might thrive with the rules in place, and therefore, that compromise is not always 'giving in' or defeat.

JOURNAL PROMPTS

1. What masks do you wear in what situations? Give them each a name.

2. For each of your masks, what has been the cost of maintaining these masks? What do you want the mask to know about the person behind that mask?

Gifted: Creativity and Intuition

It's not surprising that entrepreneurship offers a unique refuge for ADHD people. Entrepreneurs set their own rules, crafting environments that align with their needs and boundaries. Unfortunately, not everyone has the privilege to pursue entrepreneurship. It requires social and financial capital, risk tolerance, and a safety net that many don't have enough extra time or money to build. For most people, corporate roles provide stability, a regular income, and fewer existential uncertainties, even if these environments lack the flexibility ADHD people often need to thrive.

We're typically really creative and have an intuition that kind of borders on witchcraft because when we know, we know. If that's the person we're going to be with, we know. If a person we've never met before comes up to you, we get a bad vibe; we don't ignore that.

ADHDers know who the good people are and who is faking it. We often try to ignore that and rationalise it away because there isn't a way to prove it. So, we get better at listening to our intuition, but I think it's really important that we lean into that because it usually is a good warning sign for us. We need those warning signs, given that disaster frequently finds us. Honestly, even in situations where we haven't intentionally or unintentionally done anything, for whatever reason, we do find ourselves in really interesting, exciting stories that have their limits in terms of how interesting and fun they are.

Pattern Recognition: Making Value by Making Meaning

ADHD leaders are so good at seeing connections that are not obvious to others. The difference between synthesis and summary is that a summary is just telling us what happened. If we're thinking about a meeting or an event that happened, everyone knows what happened. They were there. They can read that for themselves in many cases. But synthesis is trying to give meaning to that: What does that mean, given this context? How does that relate to other events that have happened or are yet to happen?

Quickly processing and finding meaning within large amounts of data is something we're really good at. Trying to confine ourselves to the predictive or descriptive ways of analysing data, information, and knowledge in their various forms might be really limiting. Being able to synthesise means putting things together to develop opinions and likelihoods about things where there is no clear answer, or there are many opportunities and ways to look at it; things where people think they have a really good sense of what a topic is and the possibilities, but only because they haven't applied a completely different view or lens to it.

It's important to remember that our ability to synthesise does not make things more complicated; it adds more texture, context, meaning, and implications. We're not over-egging it. We are adding value by adding perspective, and that perspective could be the difference between success and failure for a team. So, we should be more open to exploring our ability to make unusual connections in our minds and also give ourselves the space and time to do that.

Generosity: Put the Oxygen Mask on Yourself First

I also suffer from some forms of toxic generosity, where I will give everything, I have to the point where it's very unhelpful. As my mother always says, 'Put the oxygen mask on ourselves first before others'. She says this largely because, as a nurse, she's thinking of the fact that by the time we put the mask on someone else, we won't have time to put it on ourselves. We're dead in less than three seconds. We didn't want it on us first, but we needed it first.

If we don't put it on ourselves first, we may save the other person, but we will definitely die. If we put the mask on ourselves first, we likely save ourselves. The odds of saving the other person don't change much, so we kind of have to accept that. Unfortunately, that is difficult for ADHD people to do because we typically have a really strong sense of justice and fairness. Perhaps being judged our whole lives for things that we don't have any control over makes us more sensitive when that's happening to other people. We want to make sure that it doesn't. The best way to protect people in the workplace is to be the boss. Only the boss really gets to stop unacceptable behaviour, whether people like it or not. That alone should be a good incentive to get ourselves into a leadership role.

Honesty: I'm Not an Asshole. I'm Just ADHD.

My focus, inflexibility, and directness have been both a blessing and a curse. When I was younger, people didn't call it precocious; they called it disrespectful (Pistoria, 2023). It's interesting how the same trait gets reframed as we age. Now, as an adult, I know that directness and integrity are often appreciated. The inflexibility? Not so much. Regardless of how other people's reactions change, I haven't. Professionally, I'm the same person I was at 12: a benevolent dictator in waiting, whether I wanted to lead or not.

I realise that for most people, this is more of an autistic trait, but ADHDer bluntness is legendary. Our literal response can come across as curt or blunt when it's simply straightforward. These misunderstandings can create tension if left unspoken and unaddressed. The worst thing about that? The ADHDer probably will have no idea about any of it.

While I think I am simply pointing out factual information, it can come across as me basically saying, 'I hate everything and everyone. ' It's fair that I take a very hard view of the world, but that isn't the same as being hard when our brain is so literal. When people think they're joking with me, they don't understand that. To me, they've just lied. They thought we were being jokey and fun, but they deceived me, and I didn't know how to lighten my response to make us feel comfortable. Why should I comfort you when we're the ones who hurt me?

It's exhausting having to nurse people through their reactions to our reaction to them being inappropriate. This stuff never gets talked about in all those leadership books. I have spoken to many neurodivergent friends about the constant vigilance of remembering to laugh at jokes we don't find funny and not laugh at those we do find funny, because that makes us look weird. In many ways, that hyper-self-awareness is eating away at our ability to connect and, more importantly, eating away at our desire to connect with others. We get to a point where we think, 'Why would I want to? I can't do this. It's too hard.

Chapter 5

Get Boring Stuff Done

Our brains can become our unfair advantage. Traits like thinking creatively, not being afraid to challenge the status quo, and having massive amounts of energy to work in short, sharp bursts—these are all things that make us dynamic and unstoppable. That's as long as we can manage our energy accordingly and aren't trying to do that every day, all day, ending up burning out or in the emergency room. If we can strike a balance, it's all good. We should 100% be doing those things to raise our profile and increase our perceived value to our employers and those we lead.

I've been super lucky that a lot of the things I've been obsessed with have correlated with things organisations see as valuable and will pay me money for, like transforming organisations, being really interested in organisational design, working on change management, and making leaders less remote and oblivious to the needs of their people. All of those things have, at some point, been professional obsessions for me, so I leaned into hyperfocus to get more done faster than my peers with a complex set of hacks and habits for productivity.

There's a reason these productivity hacks are called 'hacks' instead of solutions. It really is because they're temporary in their nature and their impact is usually short-term. Rather than obsessing over methods like the Pomodoro technique or other time management trends, it's far more effective to establish systems. And even then, it's important to accept that every routine we develop will eventually fall apart at some point. So, what we need are systems that ensure that we don't have to take action for things in our lives to work still.

For example, if we don't feel like getting up that day, that doesn't change that our kids still need to be able to get to school. Creating the systems that force our brains into getting up is essential.

I was never very good at forcing my brain to do anything, but I did get quite good at adopting the kind of hacks that looked good enough from the outside. One of the things that I did early on in my leadership career to signal competence was writing an end-of-week email at the start of the week that had in it the summary of what happened that week, what I'd learned, and what the next steps were. That was interesting as a planning device for the week to make sure I was super clear about what I was going to achieve, specifically in that week. But it was also a really useful report-back tool that I could use to send to whoever was my line manager so that even if they didn't read the email, they had some vague impression that I was organised, knew what was going on, had a plan, and was working to that plan.

Sometimes, just the impression was kind of enough.

Besides that, I often impulsively did something that no one else approved. I probably did forget to tell others what I was doing in our meeting but I had my ass covered regardless. I was able to point at some of those update emails and point out that I did say that I was going to attempt to do this thing. This was what I meant. To twist the knife, I often added the reminder that if my leaders actually read my updates, they would have known and emailed me about it two weeks ago. That's often enough to have people back down because it's got a very strong 'As I mentioned in my previous email' vibe. It definitely worked to sustain my credibility.

I made sure to colour-code everything. This actually goes for every-thing from my wardrobe (my clothes are colour-coded in the order of rainbow colours), but it also meant that I colour-coded stuff that was on my desk. I used different-coloured pens for different purposes. If I were writing verbatim notes of a meeting, I'd do that with a black pen. Then, if I were making notes about my thoughts about what someone was saying, rather than exactly what they said, I'd write that in red pen.

That's obviously become easier in some ways because now we have great tools where we can set an AI to join our meeting or hit record on an app to get those meeting notes transcribed. However, I've found that on some level, we still end up taking quite a lot of time if we want to connect what was said in the meeting to our notes and ensure that they align and that we've got a clear sense of what was going on when we wrote that note. So, I still prefer to take some physical notes when it's important that I either appear to be listening or need actually to listen for tasks assigned to me.

To be fair, I also take the transcripts or emails that people have sent me or slides that were discussed in the meeting and print them out. It's not very environmentally friendly, so I try to use recycled paper, printing on both sides, printing two things on one side—all of those things. But undefinedit's a lot easier to edit and find mistakes doing it that way with a red pen than it would be if I were just trying to look at it on the screen. My inattention to detail means that I need to find some way to make the details stick to me; they just happen to be a little bit easier for me to spot when they're not on the screen but actually in front of me.

I've also been really good at swapping, organising, and editing spoons with other people. I can generate a lot more energy from helping others than I can from doing things myself. So, if I had a document to edit, I might offer to edit someone else's document. In contrast, they edited mine because if I'm doing something for someone else, there's a lot more personal incentive for me and the value that I place in that than if I were doing it just for myself. Things that only impact me aren't really good enough to inspire consistent action.

TRY THIS: SUSTAINABLE HACKS I USE TO GET STUFF DONE

PERSONAL:

- Manage your energy, not your time. Protect your spoons for the things that matter.

- Don't assume everything is about your ADHD. Maybe you're just bad at that task. Some problems are behavioural and not neurological.

- Never skip workouts or therapy. Ever.

- Give up alcohol – it's not worth it. Our brains process it differently.

- Keep a standard bedtime and wake-up time. Mine are 21:30 and 6:00.

- Get a gaming chair because no office chair can compete with that level of comfort.

- Never have a TV in your bedroom.

- It is likely you will forget to speak to your friends and family. Pre-book time with them. My sister has a meeting invite for every three weeks on a Sunday afternoon.

- Make regular appointments for friends to come over to your home. You will magically find yourself suddenly able to clean the full house, do all the laundry, and cook lunch.

PROFESSIONAL:

- Don't spend too much time working on your weaknesses. You were hired for your strengths and spikes. The return on time investment for things you suck at is nowhere near the return for things you are great at. Your aim should be to be the best at your strengths, not to meet expectations at your weaknesses.

- Colour-code everything. I even use different colours for my notes: black for what the other person said and red for my commentary or opinion about it.

- Block time to spend in your Working Genius.

- Have an audiobook or podcast to listen to while you work on something boring. It may take longer to complete, but it will get done with something to semi-distract your brain.

- Ask other people for real deadlines and be honest about how regular or granular these need to be for you.

- Draw slides and plan memos on paper before making digital versions.

- Find body doubles. Sometimes having someone in the same physical and virtual space allows you to get more work done. You don't talk or help each other. Your mutual presence is enough.

LEADERSHIP:

- Accept that no one can take in as much information as you can or work as fast as you can. They bring other skills to the table. They don't need to duplicate yours.

- Talk about your limitations openly and hire people who are strong where you are weak.

- Do a team kick-off to discuss team norms, strengths, roles, and goals. Make commitments about how you want to communicate and when you want to be in the office. Repeat and update once a quarter.

- Always have a grown-up on the team whom you can talk freely to. The team needs to be protected from the drama and politics, but you can't cope with no one to speak to. Your friends and family care, but not that much. Designate a team member as the other adult based on their maturity and trustworthiness.

- Most people only have updates or check-ins. Both of these are 'process' meetings. You need some content meetings too. Schedule a weekly 'Ask Me Anything' session or problem-solving meeting to give the team an opportunity to test ideas and solutions with you without feeling like they are bothering you.

- Enforce a ten-minute rule. If any team member is confused about something you have asked for, they can only try to work it out for themselves for ten minutes. After that, they have to come to you for help and clarification.

- Teach the team that if I have to ask them for something, it's already late. Keep me updated to avoid disappointment for both of us.

- Ensure that team members argue and disagree with you. You hired them for a reason, so make sure they challenge your ideas. Make dissent normal.

- Find a good transcription app. Record yourself talking about everything. Download the transcripts and get your chosen AI to turn those into emails to your team or items for the shared team to-do list.

My NICER Framework

The converse is also true. There will be situations where there are topics that we really do not care about at all, making it difficult to engage with them. Maybe these are your frustrations but you can't lean into your genius for some valid reason. That's when we have to start gamifying those tasks. When we think about how to change our soundtracks—the constant narrative going through our minds—it's not always possible to completely rewire our brains to have no sense of limitation. In fact, I would argue that it's almost impossible to do that because as we achieve more, succeed more, learn more about ourselves, and get deeper into ourselves. We uncover layers of work that we still need to do on ourselves, giving rise to more fears and more limiting beliefs, as well as more opportunities and potential. So, I try to tell people that one of the narratives or soundtracks that should be going through their minds all the time is, 'How can I make things NICER?' Regardless of what limiting belief we have, we can always make things NICER. By NICER, I don't mean the word. I mean the acronym N-I-C-E-R.

N *is for* **New** — How can I make this look, sound, or work in a new way? How much dopamine can I get from **making changes**?

I *is for* **Immediate** — Could I **wait until the last minute** to do this? Can I make myself have to do it now e.g., booking dinner in two hours?

C *is for* **Consequential** — How can I **raise the stakes**? How do I make completion of this more important for others?

E *is for* **Exciting** — Can I introduce risk? Can I turn this into a competition? Can I push **beyond my comfort zone** into the unknown?

R *is for* **Rewarding** — How can I **get rewarded** after this is done? Can I add colour-coding or font alignment to soothe my brain?

NICER framework for getting stuff done

I started talking about NICER to my ADHD coaching clients as a way to explain how to get the most out of their energy and creativity:

- **N is for New:** If something is new, it is, by definition, going to spark some of that dopamine from the novelty, from the not knowing, from the sense of discovery that we have with anything new. New things also have a learning curve, so we have to concentrate much harder on getting good at them simply because we haven't done them before. For a brain that's as quick to learn as the ADHD brain is, it takes in a lot of information and stimuli simultaneously.

New things are good for the brain and a really useful way to avoid boredom that might otherwise make us careless or inattentive to details.

- **I is for Immediate:** Deadlines are our best friends. There is a reason we sometimes get a reputation for being procrastinators. Our dopamine-seeking brains are often looking for excitement. Urgency is exciting.

We can't really explain why we always leave five minutes before going somewhere if the maps app we're using says it takes five minutes to get there, right? Because obviously, there's still time to put our coat on, lock the house up, go outside, get into our car, drive to the place, find parking, and walk out. Those five minutes are never going to be sufficient to get us there.

Regardless of what the app says, although it may be the very definition of insanity, we keep making the same mistake of not being able to predict accurately how long it's going to take us to complete a certain task or arrive at a location. Snatching victory from the jaws of defeat at the last minute is too much fun.

- **C is for Consequential:** every time someone sets a false or fake deadline on something, I can't do it. It's the reason I had nine months to work on my master's thesis but only spent the last two and a half months working on that dissertation. It was because until then; the deadlines set by, say, my supervisor didn't really have a consequence for not meeting them. It's the same reason I stopped going to tutorials: I realised they weren't taking attendance; there was no negative or positive impact for me going there. So, it was inconsequential. It didn't really matter. Our brains find it difficult to do things that really have little rationale or impact, one way or the other, to do something or not do something.

- **E is for Exciting:** This one is probably the easiest because something it means is exciting but, hopefully, not destructive. But often, things like risky sexual behaviour, substance abuse, alcohol, partying, gambling, and driving fast cars are all exciting. They have an adrenaline rush associated with them; one often gets a dopamine rush from engaging in those activities. Now, we can find less dramatic, less drastic ways of making things interesting. Gamification is something that people have played with for many years. Honestly, I think every ADHD person is constantly trying to gamify their lives to make them more exciting; that helps them overcome the stagnation of boredom, which might result in people not thinking that we are as invested as they are.

- **R is for Rewarding:** This is the last one, which I added recently.

R is for Rewarding because sometimes we are doing something that is a slog. We don't necessarily want to be doing that. It's not interesting. It's not new; it's not exciting. Maybe it doesn't matter to anyone else, but for us, it's super rewarding. Here, I think about when I worked in an emergency room in a large public hospital; I was really disinterested in the main work that I was supposed to be doing, which was developing a surgeon dashboard to reduce waiting times, because I understood that surgeons did not care what I thought. Thus, it was completely inconsequential whether I made it or not; they didn't care. But for me, what was super rewarding was being able to help with the stocktake of all the medication that was in the emergency room, as well as all their consumables, like bandages, plasters, and needles. That stocktake had never been done.

They never had anyone to do it. Finding some students, rounding them up, and getting them to spend a week during that stocktake was incredibly rewarding to me, even though it wasn't particularly exciting. No one was really going to pat me on the back for that. It felt like a sense of achievement because it felt like something that was important to other people, something that I was really proud to be involved in. That's why I say that the soundtrack that should be going through our minds every time we hear something negative, every time our brain is going, 'I really don't want to do this', is to have our response ready.

TRY THIS: MAKING TASKS NICER

Choose three boring but necessary tasks you're currently avoiding. For each, brainstorm ways to make it NICER:

New: How could I approach this differently?

Immediate: How could I create urgency or deadlines?

Consequential: How could I raise the stakes?

Exciting: How could I add elements of play or challenge?

Rewarding: What meaningful reward could I connect to completion?

Implement your NICER strategies for two weeks and track completion rates compared to your normal approach.

Practical Ideas for Applying the NICER Framework

Making Work New

1. **If you aren't a manager yet**: If you have to do the same monthly report every time, try making it in the usual way and a completely different format to test with your boss. Use a new software tool, like a new generative AI bot. Ask colleagues who get your report about what they actually need from your report, rather than just copying last month's version. Volunteer for any new projects, even when they are only kind of related to your job.

2. **If you manage teams**: Spoon-swap to give a peer with complementary skills the budget review whilst you take on their project update. Work from home or a co-working space for a change in scenery. Swap responsibilities with a peer manager for one quarter. Ask your team for ideas to make any of their work new and fresh.

3. **If you are at a director or executive level**: Visit a different office location each month, with bonus points if you can work from there for a few weeks. Invite your peers or team members to run the leadership meetings you usually chair. Think about a problem from a competitor's perspective and see how they might reinvent your current solution.

Adding Urgency to Make Work Immediate

1. **If you aren't a manager yet**: Break your massive project into daily mini-deadlines. Set a timer for 25 minutes and see how much you can get done in that time. Tell your boss you'll finish a part of a deliverable by end-of-day and ask them to check in with you then.

2. **If you manage teams:** Move deadlines for things you need to review closer together rather than giving yourself time to procrastinate. Schedule weekly check-ins instead of monthly ones. Set up peer accountability where you report progress to each other daily.

3. **If you are at director or executive level:** Implement regular business reviews with your boss to showcase the work of your team. Make a commitment to family or friends that means you have to finish a daily task by a certain time to keep your promise. Allow anyone to set-up a meeting with you with 12 hours notice so that you have a reason to get more done to make-up for the lost time.

Hold Yourself Accountable with Real Consequences for Performance

1. **If you aren't a manager yet**: Connect your boring task to something that actually matters to your boss in a way that both need to be done. Ask your manager to explain why a particular task exists and what happens if it's done badly.

2. **If you manage teams**: Make an internal commitment to do something in a specific time frame. Connect individual tasks to team goals. Ask for your bonus to be linked to your performance if it isn't already. Make it clear that delays in their work affect other departments who are waiting for their output.

3. **If you are at director or executive level:** Make a public com-

mitment to do something in a specific time frame. Link every boring administrative task to the company's strategic goals and your team's master plan. Ask for a performance scorecard linking your tasks with company and customer impact.

Build the Excitement

1. **If you aren't a manager yet**: Turn data entry into a game by setting speed records. Create a competition with yourself to spot patterns in the information. Listen to a gripping podcast whilst doing repetitive tasks and reward yourself with an extra episode when your finish in record time. Use different coloured pens for different types of information.

2. **If you manage teams**: Gamify your team's targets with leader boards and prizes. Create mystery challenges where team members have to figure out solutions. Start a friendly competition between departments. Introduce elements of surprise in meetings or silly traditions that get everyone laughing.

3. **If you are at director or executive level**: Turn strategic planning into war games with scenarios and role-playing. Create innovation challenges where departments compete to solve the business problems most important to you. Use external facilitators and famous speakers to run leadership sessions differently. Raise the stakes with a commitment of your budget or salary to a specific outcome.

The Secret Source is Reward

1. **If you aren't a manager yet**: Connect boring tasks to your personal values. If you care about helping people, remind yourself how your accurate record-keeping helps colleagues find information quickly. Celebrate small wins by treating yourself with

your desired treat after completing difficult tasks. Nominate yourself or ask others to nominate you for prizes or awards.

2. **If you manage teams**: Publicly recognise team members who excel at the mundane stuff, offering them tangible and intangible incentives like store gift vouchers or mentoring opportunities. Collect and regularly share stories about how your team's behind-the-scenes work made a difference. Keep a record of problems you've solved so that you can look at the list and feel accomplished by what you have already done, not discouraged by what comes next.

3. **If you are at director or executive level:** Share success stories with the board about impact and gains. Write thought leadership about how you solved certain problems and what that help you understand what you consider a reward for a good day of work. Connect smooth operations to your personal brand as someone who makes things work.

The key thing I learned is that we can't always make work thrilling, but we can usually make it feel more worthwhile. Sometimes the reward is knowing that other people can rely on you to handle the boring stuff so they can focus on the exciting projects. That's actually quite powerful once you embrace it.

Part III
Rewriting Your Leadership Beliefs

Chapter 6

Eight Stories We Tell Ourselves About Why We Can't Lead

In the stories we tell ourselves, we're often an unreliable narrator. People generally fight against their own interests and choose to believe they can't do things before they are willing to admit they can. Here are the lies I believed about leadership ten years ago:

- We either have leadership abilities or we don't.

- There's no such thing as ethics in leadership. We do what we have to.

- Leaders are all smart or, at least, smarter than I.

- I won't get promoted unless I know someone near the top.

- Leaders don't deserve their high salaries unless they're working 20-hour days.

- Leadership is simply a better-paying version of management.

None of these beliefs was accurate. I had no evidence to support them beyond my own feelings and insecurities. I gained nothing from these beliefs except impostor syndrome and anxiety. You're probably not gaining much more than I was.

TRY THIS: What's Your Soundtrack?

Write down every belief you hold about leadership and yourself as a potential leader. For each belief, ask yourself:

- Is it true? Is there objective evidence for this belief? Would my best friend agree with my assessment?

- Where did this belief come from?

- Was this a belief someone else shared about me, or something that I assumed about what someone else thought about me?

- How do I benefit from my believing this? What does this belief cost me?

- What would be possible if I didn't believe this?

What are your limiting beliefs about leadership? These may have started as lies that other people told us, and we just internalised them and believed them. But if we want to unlock our potential as a leader, truly, we need to start to think about how we unravel these beliefs so that we can change our behaviour.

Here are some ideas I have come across coaching fellow ADHDers:

'I'm Too Sensitive to Manage Anyone'

The idea that we are too sensitive to be leaders because of rejection sensitivity dysphoria, because we experience feelings so intensely, our very clear sense of justice, our desire to be honest about things—all of that means that we might expose ourselves to more intense reactions from others, which in turn trigger more intense reactions within ourselves. But sensitivity isn't actually a bad thing in many cases.

Highly sensitive people are able to produce incredible things like works of art, for example, or are able to take on careers like caregiving, psychology, art therapy, dance, and teaching, which require some form of empathy and understanding of others to help them achieve things in their lives. So, sensitivity by itself is not a terrible thing.

Part of the reason we think it's a terrible thing is that those who would like to control our beliefs about ourselves find it very convenient to turn our strengths into weaknesses in our minds. Not being 'too sensitive' also means that we're less likely to call out the BS of a bully in the workplace or someone who's making other people feel uncomfortable simply for existing. You've already stopped to doubt whether this is a 'you' problem or a 'them' problem: Is this happening, and is this response happening because of something they're doing, or because our brain has tricked us into believing that this is terrible when it's actually totally fine?

We are not too sensitive to leadership. I would argue that we're just the right amount of sensitivity for leadership because we've all heard of or been managed by people who had 0% empathy for the situations we found ourselves in, and we know how poor that mindset is for the outcomes that employees experience. So be the good boss we never had and exercise a little bit of that sensitivity and the empathy that comes along with it.

'If They Can't Do It, Why Would I Be Able To?'

Next, we tell ourselves that we are all the same, so obviously, what is true for you must also be true for me. We need the same reasonable adjustments, so surely, our ADHD brains are all kinds of the same. Neurodivergent people are just variations on the same theme.

This kind of thinking makes it really easy to limit what we believe is possible in our lives.

Given the low employment rates for neurodiverse people, in particular those who are autistic but also those who are ADHD, it is very easy for us to imagine that certain things are out of reach. But just because other people have failed to do something does not give us any indication of our ability to do that thing. There's very little correlation between our desires and ambitions, our ability to achieve what we intrinsically want, and other people's failures.

The only link there is one that we create for ourselves when we create some sort of equivalence. That means that other people's failing makes it more likely that we too will fail, when they actually have nothing to do with us and truly should not be our model for our own abilities and limitations.

This concept relates to the soundtracks that play in our minds and the stories we tell ourselves about our competency, which may be incorrect. Even if they are correct right now, the thing that people forget is that we can change our reality. Our reality is not like our brain. It is something that we are manifesting every day.

We know that there is a significant amount of neuroscience to support the use of affirmations and manifestations in changing how we perceive our reality. As a result, we start to encounter more situations and meet more people who share our worldview and align with our existing thoughts.

If we walk into the pharmacy super grumpy and unhappy, it's super unlikely we're going to get a smile on the face of the pharmacist who serves us, as Mel Robbins points out. But if we walk in there with a huge smile on our face and a really friendly attitude, it's going to be much more difficult for the pharmacist to meet us with indifference and coldness. They may still, but the likelihood is significantly reduced simply because we have changed our own mindset and the way we interact with others.

So, this idea that the stories that we tell ourselves about ourselves are always true or always untrue is a false binary that we don't need to believe. The important thing is controlling those stories and making sure that they're intentional so that we're not accidentally killing our chances of greatness with ideas that we have created independent of the facts.

'ADHD Makes Us Bad Employees'

There are also lies that we've been told about being bad employees. A lot of this comes from our challenges with executive functioning, the set of skills that allow us to plan and manage our time and activities. Things like time blindness, a lack of object permanence, and time paralysis all of these things make it incredibly difficult to plan accurately, and often, the ADHD brain has a very short time horizon. It's capable only of thinking about the immediate outcomes of our activities.

So, if I have to file this PowerPoint report and I absolutely hate doing PowerPoint, my brain will fixate on the boredom that is coming about with that. This will lead to increased stress because I crave stimulation and rewards, which means I need to find enjoyable activities to engage in. Those fun things to do may be setting my house on fire and completely ignoring the report that needs to be filed. Sure, it'll make me feel better in the short term as I watch my house burn to the ground and try to imagine what a crazy situation I've put myself in and what an awesome story this is going to make when I rebuild my house.

It doesn't help me with the longer-term goal of filing that report, which is part of my job.

So, I won't lie to anyone and say that executive functioning challenges don't present huge barriers in terms of us being good employees. However, I would also like to point out that people who are not neurodivergent also struggle with tasks such as time management, planning activities, and understanding the effort required to complete certain tasks. That is not a specific neurodivergent quirk.

There are ways, given that a lot of this is about behaviour rather than beliefs, to change some of that behaviour and create some safeguards and scaffolding for ourselves. This support can help us have the kind of executive functioning we need at critical points, while also allowing us to lapse entirely on our ability to executive function when it is not required. We don't need to be on a hundred per cent of the time, and so if we want to take a Sunday once a month just to be our most paralysed version of ourselves, who does not do a single thing, we can do that. There is nothing to prevent us from exercising in small bursts or small aspects.

One of the things I have often done to avoid the stress of planning and following the same routine every day, such as driving to the office, is to never leave at the same time. I will try to take different routes, even if it's just turning left instead of right at one set of traffic lights. I try to listen to different playlists or different podcasts, and all of that helps trick my brain into believing that I'm not in the same kind of routine and that it's not going to get boring and that I shouldn't stress out and, therefore, look for fun in all the wrong places.

So, we can be great employees for several reasons: our creativity and energy, our commitment to justice and honesty, and our ability to get things done really quickly. The challenge of having too much attention, not too little, and being able to input a huge amount of data in a very fast period of time. Those are all things that make us great employees, plus the weird loyalty that we have to people who have given us a chance and who have seen us for more than just our neurology.

'ADHD Makes Us Bad Managers'

Similarly, all the same things that make people think we're bad employees also lead them to assume that we'd be bad bosses. I think that's particularly nonsensical given that a lot of the executive functioning that executives are expected to do, they outsource.

I had an amazing executive assistant, Debbie, who, during the COVID-19 pandemic, would plan bathroom breaks and take a five-minute stretch break several hours a day. She was very good at planning when I would have dinner and when I would go for a walk with my partner, ensuring that people didn't infringe on that time. I did zero per cent planning in those days. All I would do was check my diary that morning and every couple of hours to see what Debbie decided I should do that day.

It got to the point where Debbie was also organising some private activities, such as my charity work and board roles, not because that was her job, but because, in her words, I was disrupting her schedule by trying to plan things myself. That is the privilege of being the boss; other people get to do things like organise our lives and figure out what we need to do and when.

It's something I've also really enjoyed about having a house manager, who, for me, is the equivalent of an executive assistant at work: someone who helps with not just everyday cleaning tasks but also maintenance that needs to be done in the house.

When I needed my chimney serviced at the same time as my shower was being fixed, and I also wanted my oven cleaned and a blind mounted in my bedroom, I didn't attempt to figure out how to do all of these things myself. Instead, I went to my house manager and simply asked her to make time for those things. Regardless of whether it takes her two or three weeks to complete those tasks, it is likely to take me several times, 2, 3, or 7 months, before I actually get through that to-do list. And so, her perception of her inefficiency of taking a couple of weeks to get something done was way better than my perception of my own ability to do that without her.

We often think that we are spoiled, ungrateful, or overly privileged to receive such support because it's not a matter of life or death. We don't need it, in the minds of most people, to function. But I would argue that whatever helps us to get the best out of ourselves, whatever scaffolding and support structures we need to create so that we are able to achieve what we need to do, are not optional. They're not a luxury. They're not something we're indulging in.

At the end of the day, our ability to rise through those ranks has a huge impact on our friends and family in material and immaterial ways. It has a huge impact on the people we will lead and their future careers. It has an impact on the trajectory of our company and how likely it is to be able to continue to have good employees who want to stay because they have good bosses and, in turn, be able to create things that our clients or customers want to buy to keep us in business.

So, it is not a form of indulgence to get the kind of support that we need to help us with our executive functioning, even if it does seem a little extra or something weird to be spending money on. It is more irresponsible to allow ourselves to struggle in ways that someone else could very easily fix for us because it implies a set of limiting beliefs about what help we are entitled to versus what help is optional, and it is kind of an over-the-top aspect.

'You Need Natural Talent to Lead'

Another lie we tell ourselves is that we have to be a natural talent to accomplish something. I think this obsession with natural talent has really derailed a lot of people's self-confidence because we tend to value natural talent way more than hard work to get something right.

People often celebrate those with natural talents more than those who have worked hard to achieve something. This seems backward. I would prefer to be celebrated for the things I have worked on, the things I have put my intention and time into and achieved results that I am proud of. These are not things I was born with, which is a matter of chance, not a genetic lottery. It's about being in the right place, having geographic and economic privilege, and being at the right time, which is a chronological privilege.

For instance, if a Black person were born in the 1800s, it would be tough luck if they were a good leader. They were never going to win any elections or run any companies. Being a natural talent for leading people probably isn't going to be that useful in the long run. Many of those natural talents peak very early. Because they had the talent, they didn't really work that hard at getting super good at it. They're already successful, so they might think they don't have to listen to other leaders' advice, and they don't need to read any books.

This results in a form of complacency that makes it much more difficult for them to catch up in terms of discipline, skills, or mindset. The motivation and the focus to keep going when we know something is going badly don't usually manifest for those whose talents were discovered super early and were praised as being the best in the class. They might not be able to get any further than that and might have all sorts of stories they've told themselves about why or why not. But it's also possible they're just not that smart, and that is not generally an impediment to being able to work, make money, and be successful in their career path.

Serena Williams 100% had natural talent as a tennis player, but she could not have risen through the ranks and become the legend that she did on talent alone. That was never going to work. She also had to invest in her fitness, her mindset, her strategic thinking, her problem-solving abilities, and her emotional resilience, and none of that had to do with natural talent.

It was the sole function of working hard towards the goals she wanted to achieve that paid off for her a hundred per cent. I think it is very hard to find anyone who is simply coasting off their natural talent at the highest level of their profession or their vocation without putting extra work in.

Just because we weren't born with the ability to do something does not mean that we will be bad at it or that we can't learn to do it.

In every profession, some people excel because they work hard, and some people excel because they're smart enough to be able to wing it and work less. People who've done a combination of both are the real unicorns. If we can be anything, be a unicorn.

'I'm Just the Token Disabled/ND Team Member'

Being the only one of any minority in a workplace may make people question our competence, expertise, and right to be there by default. They may think we are a diversity hire, i.e., a person who holds their position solely because of their demographic. Newsflash: if we're a minority, we're going to have to deal with that doubt anyway. The only difference is that we would have genuinely earned the privilege of being underestimated or disrespected by our peers and leaders. Why, then, are we so afraid of being the DEI hire? If we're going to deal with the same problematic behaviour regardless of our actual skills or experience, why not skip the part where we have to do all the hard work to get there?

Do you want to know a secret? I would love to be a DEI hire. I suffer greatly for my intersectionality, so it would be nice to be compensated well for it, too. I daydream about being incompetent yet still keeping my job. I want to be able to suck at my job and get paid to leave it so that I focus on 'spending more time with my family'. Even better if it means that I don't have to mask through any of that because I'm the autistic diversity hire, so people expect me to be super autistic by default. I want the excuse for all my bad behaviour also to be the thing I am getting paid for.

However, that's not the reality we face. On this timeline, men are promoted based on potential, while women are promoted based on perfection. Members of certain clubs are able to bypass application questions and proceed directly to job offers because they know the right person. Doing a good job is sometimes entirely optional.

Similarly, doing a good job doesn't actually guarantee that we get rewarded for that or that we get to keep that gainful employment. Who we are and who we know matter, whether we are the diversity hire or not. We still have to do the work and suffer through the small talk meetings that could have been sent as emails instead, even if no one thinks we earned our place. So don't stress if we feel like we didn't earn our seat at the table. Plenty of people didn't. Our job is to keep our seats so that others have a neurodivergent leader in the room where the important stuff happens.

'There's Only One Right Way'

Similarly, if we don't do something in an X way, it does not mean that we can't do it or that we will be unsuccessful. Often, people believe that their way of doing things is the best way to do things. In fact, if they're more arrogant, it becomes the only way of doing things.

That is something I'm quite against, which is why I prefer to use this book as an apprenticeship rather than a blueprint. I love the idea of different things working for different people, and I'm simply sharing that being a little bit more Machiavellian certainly helped me protect my team and protect their jobs much better than the alternative of being a little bit more chill and a little bit more relaxed about what was happening in the business and what impact it had on the people who worked for me. So, if we don't do it my way, that does not mean that we cannot do it.

Similarly, if it hasn't worked yet, that doesn't mean that it won't. There is no expiration date on success, and no one should make us feel as though we're running an imaginary race against our future selves, where we're trying to outpace them and be better than whatever they're trying to achieve. We are not in conflict with our future selves. You're in collaboration, we're in a partnership, we're helping each other. So, there is no reason to punish our current self for our past self's failures, and there is no reason to hamstring our future self by having our current self so obsessed with what has or hasn't happened in the past that they're unable to look forward to the future.

Something I often tell my mentees is: do not let a past version of us make decisions for a future version of ourselves. I think this happens all the time when people forget that they've improved at something. There might have been a time when we felt incredibly insecure about our ability to present in front of others, but we spent a year working on that and got much more comfortable and competent in doing that. It would then not make sense for us to decline a speaking opportunity because we believed we would be nervous, as we've already worked on that aspect and changed the reality about our present self. It was only our past self that couldn't have done that, and a failure to acknowledge that means that our future self misses out on opportunities that could be truly awesome.

'You Can't Be What You Can't See'

The penultimate lie, which I think we tell women in particular all the time, but also people from minority ethnic groups, is 'we can't be what we can't see.'

Unfortunately, we do not owe anybody else our diagnosis or our disclosure. No leader has to tell us that they are ADHD or become a poster child for what we want to achieve in our own lives. I think this further reinforces the superpower label applied to ADHD, which just isn't that helpful for ordinary people struggling with their disability.

I also think it puts way too much pressure on people who get to those positions, like me, to try and be a perfect example, because that has an impact on every other person who's like me that might come after me.

I think that if we want to be a pioneer, if we want to do something different from what we have seen in our life, from what our friends have done, from what our family expects, that requires doing something new. And often, that thing, while it might not be new to others, is new to you, and we might not have a role model for how to do that. We might just be figuring it out as we go, building the plane as we fly it, and that's totally fine because other people have been given the privilege of being able to do that.

It would be incredibly weird if we went to a redheaded White man in our office and asked whether he feels like he can't be in leadership because there's not a sufficient number of redheads in leadership. That sounds crazy. So, why do we make it so important that other minority identities and characteristics need to be exhibited at a senior level before we believe that they are accepted in a company or that we can be at a senior level with some of those same characteristics?

Unravelling these lies, these limiting beliefs, is perhaps the most important work we can do on our leadership journey. Don't let them hold us back from being the leaders we can become and the leaders our teams need us to be.

Chapter 7

Fake It to Make It.

This is going to sound fairly autistic, but I feel like the phrase 'fake it till we make it' would more accurately be described as 'make it until we no longer need to fake it'. I get that that's not as catchy, but it is a lot more specific. Central to the idea of 'fake it till we make it' is the idea that even if someone feels like an impostor, it doesn't really matter. They just have to shut down the inner critic that accuses them of being an impostor and keep doing the work regardless of the internal soundtrack of limiting beliefs we have stuck on repeat.

Research paints a clear picture: about 70% of people will experience impostor syndrome at least once, but those of us with ADHD are particularly susceptible. Why? Partly because we spend our lives assuming we are the problem, regardless of the situation. Years of masking, people-pleasing and accommodation gradually erode our self-esteem, creating fertile ground for impostor feelings to flourish. I think of three types of impostor syndrome in relation to ADHD: The Perfectionist Imposter ADHDer, The Superhuman ADHDer, and the 'Shame by Comparison' Imposter ADHDer.

Regardless of whether we identify with these types or others, for the ADHD leader, it doesn't really matter. I always recommend just accepting that you feel like an impostor and moving on. At a certain point, there is so much evidence of your competence that irrationally feeling like an impostor is difficult to shake. So, we may as well do cool/scary things and feel impostors rather than not doing cool/scary things and feeling like an impostor anyway.

The Perfectionist Impostor ADHDer

The link between perfectionism and impostor syndrome is kind of obvious. We set these wildly high standards and then become our own harshest critics. Simultaneously, we doubt our achievements and live in constant fear of being 'found out' as frauds. This toxic combination is especially common among high-achievers with ADHD.

The perfectionist flavour of impostor syndrome is particularly devious because it's driven by the dopamine hit we get from achieving perfection. I set standards for myself that would make Olympic judges weep, and when I inevitably fall short, I'm convinced I'm an absolute fraud, even if I missed by the smallest margin. I tie my entire self-worth to what I accomplish, which is a dangerous game for an ADHD brain that's already prone to inconsistency.

For the perfectionist, competence is never enough. Achievement doesn't even register unless it's spectacular enough to silence every critic who ever doubted you.

The real question, though, is who are we actually trying to impress? Some perfectionists achieve incredible things precisely because they've set standards so lofty that others can't reach them. Others might wonder if we're faking our impostor syndrome because logically, how could someone so objectively brilliant be so utterly blind to their own competence that they need an endless stream of achievements to prove their worth?

This is essentially the definition of the anxious, overachieving, insecure professional. It's no accident that many end up in top-tier consulting, where firms absolutely thrive on perfectionist impostor syndrome. These organisations get employees who willingly work impossible hours, happily ignore their outside responsibilities, and practically glow from the tiniest scrap of praise. We work ourselves to the bone for minimal validation because proving our competence to respected colleagues feels almost narcotically satisfying.

Unfortunately, consulting companies exploit this by offering tiny crumbs of praise buried under mountains of criticism, perpetuating the myth that someday we'll reach a magical status where our competence will never again be questioned. That status is entirely fictional.

When we consider intersectionality, this reality is even harsher. No matter how much we achieve, certain people will never see it as proof of our competence. They'll continue believing we only got there because of demographic factors. I think we'll know we've achieved true workplace equity when diversity hires can be mediocre at their jobs without consequence (more on this later). (Many) women and ethnic minorities in Western workplaces get promoted based on perfection, whilst (many) white men often advance based on potential. Women's potential gets disregarded because what matters is whether they've already proven themselves perfect and how willing they are to continue that performance, even when there's no objective standard they can ever meet. Let's also not forget that intersectionality puts even white men at risk: those from the North of England, those with learning disabilities, those who are not heterosexual, and (surprise!) those with ADHD all understand the struggle of perfection being the only option is a workplace that expects you to fail.

These perfectionist ADHDers need a gentle reality check and to ask themselves: why is good enough not enough for us? Why do we judge our imperfections as unforgivable and give everyone else a second or third chance? At what point do we accept that achieving absolute perfection in any task, activity, service, or product is not just unrealistic but also a ton of additional emotional labour? This side quest for perfection steals time from innovation, iteration, feedback, reflection, and fun.

The most liberating day of my professional life was when I realised that 'good enough' was actually good enough. Try it, it's great for your skin.

TRY THIS: BE INTENTIONALLY IMPERFECT

I found that picking one low-stakes and low-risk situation to practice being imperfect really helped me. I chose team meetings and now encourage all my coaching clients to lower their standards for saying intelligent or valuable things in meetings. Women in particular often do not speak up because the conversation is flowing rapidly. They cannot see where the gap is. In financial services, construction, and many other industries, I have worked in, it is typically men talking and talking over you. You might have an idea of what to say, but do not know how to interject. With ADHD, you may have a complex about interrupting because you get accused of it so often. Then someone else says something vaguely similar to what you were going to say, and you think, "The moment has passed. I'd better just be quiet".

What I remind my clients is that senior executives will not remember that you said something silly. Let us be honest. John, Matthew, Steve, and Mark probably said something unremarkable in the meeting last week. Everybody listened, nodded politely, and moved swiftly to the next point. They were never penalised for it.

The same is true for you, but what people will remember is that those gentlemen spoke and you did not. They had opinions, and you did not. For better or worse, this is a significant marker of perceived competence in corporate and professional spaces: your ability to articulate your thoughts and have a perspective that you stand by.

This can be particularly challenging for those of us with ADHD. We might be processing information differently or struggling to find the right moment to jump into fast-moving conversations. Sometimes we hesitate because we are not sure if our thoughts are fully formed or relevant. Other times, we might blurt something out without thinking it through and then feel embarrassed.

But here is the truth: people with ADHD often have unique insights precisely because we think differently. Our lateral thinking and ability to make unexpected connections can be invaluable in strategic discussions. So, lower the bar on what you think is smart enough to say in meetings. Lower expectations of ourselves often lead to better results for everyone.

The Superhuman ADHDer

What I call 'superhuman impostor syndrome' affects those of us who believe we must do everything ourselves, working twice as hard as everyone else to prove we are not impostors. Unlike regular perfectionists who chase a particular standard because they believe it is correct, we are trying to reach that standard completely alone, without assistance. The standard does not have to be perfect, but our approach involves a toxic individualisation and rejection of help.

This superhuman impostor type overcompensates by taking on excessive responsibilities, which inevitably leads to burnout. We avoid asking for help because we view it as a weakness. I blame schools for teaching us this. When everything is a test, asking for help feels like cheating.

We have been taught that needing others makes us less competent, despite countless examples proving otherwise. Look at successful pop stars, scientists, or Olympic athletes. They all have teams. They might be running their own races or conducting their own experiments, but they rely on peers, mentors, coaches, managers, and agents who create the support network, making their extraordinary results possible.

I often tell people that women would be more likely to reach CEO positions more often if they had wives. They lack someone to manage all their domestic responsibilities and ensure their household runs smoothly, so they can focus on conquering the professional world. They must juggle domestic responsibilities alongside professional and social obligations, creating an almost impossible burden. Many successful male CEOs have someone managing their domestic challenges, contributing to social requirements like hosting dinner parties, and providing emotional support as a cheerleader, thought partner, and comforter. Without these support systems, many women struggle to progress further because doing everything alone is simply unsustainable. It is not that surprising that my first CEO position was when I was 24 and just married to a man who was committed to my career and the idea that it would lead to his early retirement.

There is tremendous value in asking for help even when we think we do not need it, and this benefit might mostly be for others. In Southern Africa, there is a concept called Ubuntu, which essentially means a person is not complete without other people. It recognises our fundamental need for others to accomplish things. The saying goes: if you want to go fast, go alone; if you want to go far, go together. My experience has been somewhat mixed. I found I could go faster with other people, but even further when working by myself. The difference was that working alone led me down a much more painful path filled with cycles of burnout, exhaustion, disillusionment, and bitterness.

With proper support networks, I moved more quickly because I had more energy. I did not exhaust myself doing everything alone and having support allowed me to focus on my strengths rather than struggling with my weaknesses, which preserved my energy and capabilities. Staying in my zone of genius became possible only through collaboration.

Superhuman impostors often fall into thinking traps like overgeneralisation (one mistake means I am a failure), all-or-nothing thinking (anything less than perfect is worthless), and catastrophising (if I ask for help, everyone will know I am incompetent).

TRY THIS: SYSTEMATIC DELEGATION

Start small with delegation. Choose one task you typically do yourself that could reasonably be done by someone else. This might be scheduling meetings, proofreading documents, checking that something was sent, following up with other departments, or researching information for a project.

Before delegating, write down exactly what you are worried will go wrong if someone else does this task. Be specific. Are you worried about quality? Timing? That they will not understand your standards? Most of our delegation-related fears are based on assumptions rather than evidence.

Now delegate that one task for something of medium importance and low risk. Give it to your most competence team member along with clear instructions, a definition for when the task is 'done', and deadlines. Check in once, but resist the urge to micromanage or take it back. When it is completed, assess: was the outcome actually as bad as you feared? How many of your fears actually manifested? What did you accomplish with the time you saved?

The goal is not to prove that your team can do things better than you can. Maybe they can't. That's irrelevant. The goal is to prove you can achieve more by working smart rather than working solo. Once you see evidence that delegation can work without the sky falling, gradually expand to other areas.

The 'Shame by Comparison' Imposter ADHDer

The tendency for us ADHDers to compare ourselves more frequently or intensely with others is rooted in our generally lower self-esteem, emotional dysregulation, and challenges with accurate self-perception. In much of the research, we frequently display inaccurate overestimation or underestimation of our abilities. This variability in self-awareness may make comparing ourselves to others the logical go-to strategy for gauging our 'real' competence. ADHD people then often feel like frauds because they see others' success as evidence of their own inadequacy.

I suspect that this comparison-fuelled form of impostor syndrome is something we create and impose on other people rather than what they have done to themselves. I think it already starts in formal education systems in primary school, where we spend a lot of time comparing children's performance to each other rather than looking at that individual child's performance in the context of who they are. It is easier to say, 'Well, kids with this grade tend to do this well. Other people in the class are doing this. Why is our kid not doing that?' Then, take each child as an individual and assess them based on where they are, not relative to their peers, but relative to themselves and how much progress they are making.

This is another reason why I ignored some of the more problematic aspects of the company in favour of truly loving my management consulting work in the early years. There was no comparison until the partner application stage. I could progress as fast as I was ready to progress, regardless of how other people were doing. There was no limit or quota on the number of people who could move to the next level and get promotions. When we were ready, we got a promotion, if that was in six months, awesome. If that was in two years, fantastic, as long as we were under the threshold for 'up or out'.

That really spurred a different level of focus on my own success, and I completely ignored everyone around me. To be honest, every time I tried to bring people together and find ways to compare each other and contrast notes in helpful and productive ways, it never quite worked out for me. In many cases, other women rejected that, partly because there was a perception that if they helped someone else succeed, they would fail as a result.

I once tried to rally the junior women of my office so that we could work towards better conditions and better performance. We knew the men all played football together on Sunday with the male partners. We knew we weren't invited. It seemed logical to me that we could help each other, coach each other, and support each other. For my efforts, a fellow junior woman reported me to a senior partner for being 'anti-man' and trying to cause trouble for no reason. That partner's advice? 'Forget them. It will be faster for you to get promoted without them. You can outlast them,'

That kind of zero-sum game is fuelled by this idea that every workplace becomes some kind of weird Highlander situation where 'there can be only one' woman or one Black person or one gay man on a team, in an organisation, on a panel, or winning a prize.

The reason for that has nothing to do with competence/incompetence by comparison and everything to do with our desire to gatekeep success and achievements; to make other people feel they do not deserve them.

Someone who is a genius, therefore, feels they are not because the people around them must be so much smarter. It is certainly something I experienced when I was in university, having friends who were winning Rhodes scholarships or international debating tournaments, and getting amazing internships at Goldman Sachs, McKinsey, or Bain while I was just plotting along, trying to get up in time for lectures. I did not really understand how to study and found formal academia really difficult before medication gave me this magical ability to concentrate on one thing at a time.

I felt like a fraud in that group of friends simply because everyone was so wildly successful. I was never going to earn a full ride scholarship from a historic foundation and had no prospects of going to an international university for a graduate degree. It was just a completely different vibe.

On some levels, I thought I just was not that smart in comparison to many of my friends. What I have come to realise, though, is that there are different types of genius and different types of giftedness. There is a real difference between being gifted and being a genius in terms of IQ. Giftedness encapsulates all sorts of things that IQ does not: problem-solving, creativity, and empathy. All of those things are really important for being successful in life, but not necessarily encapsulated in what we call an IQ test. The irony is that by trying to appear superhuman, we create the very conditions that prevent us from reaching our potential.

The most successful ADHD leaders I know have learned to build teams that complement their unique brains rather than trying to do it all alone. I missed out on years of being able to cultivate my giftedness simply because I discounted it and its existence, looking at others and thinking they were just inherently smarter or more gifted than I was. The only person I was fooling was me.

TRY THIS: A MAP OF WHO YOU WANT TO BE

My friend, Anthony Gribben-Lisle, introduced me to this 360 model that he often uses with his coaching clients. It's pretty simple, and I found it works well for getting you out of the comparison doom spiral trap.

You start by drawing a compass and placing four different people at the four points:
- *At North (Your Inspiration), put someone who inspires you without making you feel completely inadequate. This needs to be someone you can actually learn from, rather than someone who makes that voice in your head go mental about how you'll never be good enough.*

> • *At South (Your Warning), stick someone who exhibits traits you absolutely do not want to replicate. This isn't about being nasty about them. It's just having a clear reminder of behaviours you've decided are not for you. Think of them as your "never again" person.*
> • *East and West (Your Safe Peers) are for two peers you feel safe comparing yourself to. These should be people you work well with and learn from without feeling threatened or weirdly competitive. The kind of people where you can look at their progress and think "fair play" rather than wanting to cry into your pillow.*
>
> *Once you've got these four people mapped out, you've created your own reference points. You're not randomly comparing yourself to every person on LinkedIn who seems to have their life sorted. You've got your specific compass. The external 'threats' feel much less overwhelming because you've intentionally chosen who matters for your development.*
>
> *It makes the whole journey way more manageable.*

Systems to Project the Competence We May Not Feel

Regardless of whether we have our acts together or not, we need to get better at pretending to have our acts together. While we probably don't, and let's be honest, this is true of most adults, it's crucial to project confidence. Many of us would love to say that we are always on top of things, that our routines run really well, that we know what's happening in the workplace, and that we have a well-thought-out professional development plan. But for most people, that's just not the reality.

Most people are just kind of taking the opportunities that come up as they come up rather than strategically positioning themselves throughout the world. I certainly had a very squiggly career; that was not intentional in any way. I just took the jobs that people gave me, hoping that they would lead to other jobs. It wasn't that I had this massive amount of choice or intentionally made a choice to do a transformation project, a strategy project, then a people thing. I just had leaders who understood the versatility that I could offer a team with a different brain that was capable of doing many different things very well and many other things very poorly. The key was being able to channel that skill profile in the right way.

But the other part, is that I was particularly good at pretending to have my shit together, creating the kinds of systems and routines to make that work. I think a lot of that has to do with home life, to be honest, how we structure our personal life so that we have enough time to refresh our 'spoons', exercise appropriately, do meditation therapy, take medication if we choose to, and engage in energy healing if we choose to. All of those bits help us build systems that last longer than hacks.

The trick to the stealthy productivity of hacks is that it's not really about dishonesty or faking anything. It's about projecting confidence, even when we feel unsure. People who are terrible at their jobs don't usually know it, so if you're feeling imposter syndrome, that is a good sign that you are no imposter. Everyone is also figuring it out as they go, and that doesn't make them fakes.

You realise that over time that evolution makes the 'hacks' and 'pretending' become less necessary. I often tell my ADHD coaching clients: You'll reach a point where we've made it, and suddenly, you don't need to fake anything anymore. No one truly has all the answers, no matter how put-together they seem. By putting systems in place and showing up consistently, even on days when we feel like we don't have it in us, we're not just pretending. You're building the foundation for genuine competence and resilience. It's mostly about owning our progress, trusting our abilities, and recognising that, yeah, we've got this. Maybe not all the time, but enough to keep moving forward.

Chapter 8

Never Be Realistic About Your Prospects for that Leadership Role

I hear the obvious pushback to all of the above: What is the likelihood that you're going to be able to choose a role that fits your working genius? How realistic is it to always be able to choose a team with the right mix? Why should anyone believe that they can get away with just ignoring their development goals?

If we do not believe in our own agency and capability to make unlikely things happen, I think we need to get better at gaslighting ourselves. Yes, I said gaslighting.

Tactical self-delusion to overcome doubt and impostor syndrome is the only kind of gaslighting that I fully support.

If I had been realistic about my chances of working at the world's top consulting firm, moving to the UK when I went to schools where kids threw knives at each other, becoming a director at an investment bank with no investment banking experience, or leading any part of a mega-merger... well, none of those things would have happened. They are statistically unlikely given my profile and demographics, so accomplishing so much from such a low base pretty much makes me a unicorn. There are many of us unicorns out there, and I like to think that at least half of them are ND. I get my unicorn tendencies from my mother, who also happens to have undiagnosed, but laughably obvious, ADHD.

Born in Soweto to a domestic worker, she was the only woman and only Black executive in every boardroom. She was always the least-paid, most disrespected member of the Board, but that is no surprise given that this was not even a decade after the end of Apartheid. I'm also fairly sure that she is very ADHD after careers as a nurse, high-end boutique owner, communications executive, B&B owner, dry cleaner, travelling sales rep, news anchor, spin doctor, real estate agent, and caterer... I could keep going. She has had the most ADHD of ADHD squiggly career paths.

Despite her abundant skills and tenacity, people constantly disrespected her. Much of the reason why she changed jobs so quickly and had so many side hustles was that people either doubted or blocked her. She didn't let that slow her down. She just moved on to the next idea.

I firmly believe that I could never have done what she did in terms of facing such intense scrutiny and discrimination. I remember that I would often spend my weekends playing in corporate office parks because there was no one else to look after my sister and me while my mom worked over the weekends. I remember attending board meetings after school because she didn't have time to drop me off. I sat in one where they discussed how to avoid complying with affirmative action quotas. These were the beginnings of the DEI initiatives that the South African government was implementing to address inequalities in the corporate sector.

This board of directors was having a conversation about how to get out of that. It never really occurred to me at that moment that they were essentially asking the question of how to get fewer people who looked like my mother or me into that boardroom.

I thought representation didn't matter only because I'd had representation. So, for me, seeing her as the only woman or the first woman to make it was enough. I could get there because she was there. She couldn't really afford to have impostor syndrome, so neither could I. Any wavering in her self-belief or her ability to power through difficult situations would've been a complete disaster.

She is a daily reminder to me that sometimes we can't afford to be realistic about our chances. Being a little delusional can sometimes go a long way.

Sometimes, there are situations where we cannot afford to indulge in any negativity about ourselves. I say 'indulge' because there is some aspect of us that really likes to wallow in certain difficulties. It is much easier to stay stuck than it is to get moving. It's much easier to keep the loop of negative thoughts and blame ourselves and feel guilty, which then leads to more negative thoughts about ourselves. Those loops are extremely easy to get stuck in; I don't say 'super easy' as if people want to get stuck in them. I'm not even saying that people consciously do it. I just feel that we are always going to be our own harshest critics, usually more critical of ourselves than anyone else is likely to be. If someone is in a situation where everybody is actually likely to be harsher on them than they are on themselves, we have no choice but to reset the balance. Mentally, we can rate ourselves far above their expectations, partly because meeting their standards often means underperforming and falling short of our true potential. Additionally, once negative thoughts and doubts begin to creep in, they can undermine our confidence and hold us back.

Doubt causes hesitation. Hesitation leads us to feel risk averse. Risk adversity creates fear, and that fear keeps us stuck in whatever role, whatever level, whatever box, and whatever lane we've been put in because we fear what will happen if we dare to be bigger than the space that we have been allocated. Sometimes, even making an inch of progress was a fight. We lost a lot of ourselves, a lot of our energy, a lot of our excitement for our work in trying to get that inch. When we arrive, it sometimes feels like a very small plot, perhaps not worth the effort that went into creating it. So, I love that my mother essentially had a cult-like obsession with her own career. I like that she treated herself like her favourite football team and was going to support herself big time. Win or lose, have the same enthusiasm that people have for their favourite actor or their favourite musician, regardless of whether they release a good album or a bad movie. They are supporting the team no matter what. We don't forget every good thing they've done when they happen to do something wrong.

We should offer ourselves the same grace and resist allowing the death spiral of self-doubt to take over. We know that it's not a productive way to use our time. We know that that's not the way that we're going to change our situations or circumstances, yet still, it's so hard to break out of that. Try anyway.

JOURNAL PROMPTS

1. *Where might a little 'tactical delusion' about your chances of success be helpful in your current situation? How could it help?*
2. *How is a past version of yourself making decisions for your future self? What growth aren't you acknowledging?*
3. *When has impostor syndrome held you back from attempting something you were actually qualified for?*
4. *Whose voice do you hear when you doubt yourself? Is it yours, or someone else's criticism, you've internalised? Does it come with wearing one of your masks? Why do you feel the need to mask?*

5. How might you set yourself an ambition that takes you beyond these limits without seeming impossible?

Part IV
Mastering the Behaviours of an ADHD Boss

Chapter 9

Ration Your Spoons

Working with your natural energy patterns rather than against them is critical for ADHD leaders. What might surprise neurotypical colleagues is that our energy often thrives under conditions they find stressful. Last-minute, unreasonable requests from clients are my idea of a good time. They energise me, even if the time available is running out rapidly.

Conversely, the conditions that our NT colleagues find grounding or energising, like consistent routines, long stretches of time before deadlines, and documented plans, may kill all the energy we start the day with. Another way of thinking about energy is mentally switching 'energy' for 'spoons.'

The Spoons Concept is a useful analogy for understanding why energy management is more important than time management and how you can efficiently use up your energy. This concept originally came from the chronic fatigue community and people who had long-term disabilities to explain how their energy might be depleted over the course of a day.

Imagine the following: at the start of the day, you have one hundred spoons. Everything that you need to do that day requires that you give away a certain number of spoons. The specific number of spoons required for each task differs from person to person based on your interests, skills, experiences, and context. If you have to take a shower, let's pretend that you love showering. The hot water is great. So it only takes you three spoons to do that. After that and breakfast (another three spoons), you have to go on a long commute to your office in the city, and that's pretty crappy. Having to do that burns 15 spoons because you're travelling during rush hour, it's very stressful, and it takes a lot out of you to not have a meltdown an hour in.

You go through the whole day. Every activity, from making some photocopies to getting lunch with your work friends, continues to take a certain number of spoons. At the end of the day, you hope that you have two or three spoons left so that you can wash your face and get into bed. Unfortunately, sometimes there are no spoons left, and you just fall asleep on the sofa. You didn't have the spoons to get up, wash your face, brush your teeth, and crawl into bed.

This concept of finite spoons is helpful as an idea I use to explain to people when I can't do things. I'm not too tired exactly. It's not even that I don't feel like doing something. I just no longer have the capacity to do that thing. I would explain to a previous boss that if he wanted me on stage for a two-hour client event, that was fine, but then I wouldn't be able to come in the next morning at 8:00 AM. Initially, he was quite confused about how the two things were related. I explained that the number of spoons that it took for me to go on stage and talk to people is close to 50 spoons. I need the time to replenish those spoons, and sleeping alone won't do that. To replenish spoons, I might need to work on a complex problem with my team, go on a podcast, or talk to my sister.

If I were just attending the event, that would have only been five spoons because I wouldn't need to perform, mask, or be concerned that I was saying semi-interesting stuff. I could just show up. He learned that our shared goal should be to work out how to spend as few spoons as possible on as many activities as possible. Washing the dishes may take the same number of spoons as a Pilates class, a coaching call, and a walk with my dog. They cost the same number of spoons, which makes me far less likely to choose the fun stuff that I can do more of, rather than the one task that I don't want to be doing anyway.

That is why shifting from time management to energy management is like a permission slip to believe in our own capacity to get things done when we need to. Time still exists, obviously, but it doesn't become the thing you are trying to control or a stick to beat yourself into submission with.

I used that stick very liberally early in my career. That approach just led to feelings of incompetence and guilt about my inability to know whether I would be able to work 12 hours or two on any given day. I've gotten better at keeping track of how many spoons activities take and planning my work accordingly. I know that if I have a meeting at 15:00, I may end up in task paralysis and be unable to do anything else until 15:00. That's inefficient, so I schedule my meetings for first thing in the morning when I am most energised and won't lose a day to involuntary inaction. My natural work rhythm involves intense bursts of hyperfocus to meet deadlines, followed by long periods of recovery. When I don't fight my brain on that, I produce better work in less time overall, even if the distribution of that work looks different.

One other advantage of using spoons to plan work: we consistently underestimate the time it will take to complete a task. We are rarely surprised that something we didn't want to do takes a lot of energy to complete. Our spoon estimates are much more accurate, so our plans become more realistic when we stop trying to make the timing make sense. Strict time management keeps us stuck in a cycle of lateness, procrastination, shame, and panic when we inevitably fail to manage our time consistently. Energy management allows us to stop asking, 'How can I make myself work like everyone else?' and start asking, 'How can I use my spoons strategically to allow my brain to perform at its best?.' There is no shame in how many spoons we need to get things done. It is understood that it is variable by person and by day. That might be the permission your brain needs to stop stressing about how you spend your time and embrace a different kind of efficiency.

JOURNAL PROMPTS

1. What activities consistently energise you? How can you incorporate more of these into your job?

2. What activities reliably deplete you? Can they be delegated, automated, eliminated, or restructured?

3. When during the day do you naturally experience your highest energy levels? Are you scheduling the most important stuff for those times?

4. What boundaries do you need to protect your energy from unnecessary depletion?

Chapter 10

Redefine 'Good Enough'

As we get more senior and work becomes more political, we often need to redefine what 'good' means and almost always need to redefine what 'good enough' means. Are you good at your job if you are a good manager or more of a leader? Is it better to work to burnout or work your team into burnout instead? Only you can decide.

To do this, I want to encourage you to think about what others have valued about you and, just as importantly, what you value in yourself. Look beyond the obvious stuff. In my case, colleagues appreciated my skill in quickly understanding, synthesising, translating information, and adapting my communication style to suit technical, commercial, or simple language, depending on the audience. As I grew more senior, this skill became even more valuable, especially in bridging business and technology. It's worth noting that, as an executive (and in any role where we are leading but not necessarily managing the operations), much of our impact is exerted through influence rather than direct authority, which is especially true when working with peers or their reports – people over whom we have no formal control. Success in these dynamics relies heavily on personal relationship influence.

Interestingly, while others valued my translation skills, it wasn't the thing I most appreciated about myself. I got more satisfaction from my creativity, my ability to solve problems in unconventional ways, and my ability to make documents not only impactful but visually compelling.

When I focused too much on the things people loved about me and bought into their hype, it was difficult to ignore the things they hated. If I believed the hype, why shouldn't I believe the haters? This would have been okay if I was only getting feedback or a performance review once or twice a year. Instead, every week I had a formal feedback session with my manager. Things changed rapidly in even one week. One day, I was the darling of the consulting world. The next, my model has a mistake and everyone is scrambling until midnight to find and fix the problem. You can't stay regulated with those highs and lows. I realised quickly that I was going to lose my sanity and self-esteem, if I based my definition of a good day or a job well done on what other people decided to think about me on that specific day.

What I needed was a way to maintain a sense of accomplishment and self-worth outside of the volatile cycles of wins and setbacks. I realised I needed something stable, consistent, and under my control. This way, even during challenging projects, tough team dynamics, or when appreciation was hard to come by, I'd still have a reliable sense of achievement. It had to be something tangible that I could assess regularly. Waiting for quarterly performance reviews was not going to sustain me through the weekly grind.

I chose kindness. Not because it was expected—quite the opposite, in fact. The corporate culture I was in tolerated (often revered) those who were merely technically excellent, even if they were indifferent or even unkind to colleagues. I'd like to believe this is changing, with less tolerance for brilliant jerks, but I'm not convinced. More likely, we've simply become more lenient towards people with particular spikes in certain areas, even if they disregard or mistreat those around them.

What I valued was the opportunity to defy this norm: to bring kindness into the workplace, even when I didn't have to.

At the end of each day, regardless of whether a client was pleased or if I got recognition from a partner, I could look back and ask myself: 'Was I kind today?' I'd assess whether I approached my interaction challenges with kindness, regardless of the context or my mood. Eventually, this became the only metric that truly mattered to me, making the highs and lows of the job much easier to navigate. My sense of stability grew because I had something under my control to focus on. I no longer had to worry each week whether I was hitting some external, shifting benchmark of value.

It's important to distinguish value from strengths. For instance, if someone asked me about my strengths in a feedback session, I wouldn't list kindness. While I consider it a skill, it doesn't capture the essence of a professional strength in a corporate environment. To be clear, if kindness is our top strength, a corporate setting may not be the right environment for you. I certainly haven't abandoned the importance of kindness – far from it. In everyday life, we're socially pressured to be kind. Kindness, moreover, has moral and ethical implications for most people. Kindness isn't about being nice. Sometimes, kindness requires delivering hard truths or making sure someone is fully aware of a difficult reality, even if it's uncomfortable.

If I were to describe my professional value, I'd phrase it less as 'being kind' and more as 'being able to identify what people need and giving it to them in a way that helps them move forward'. This is less traditional coaching, which leaves space for personal growth discovery, but more of an educational approach that provides a solid foundation of guidance and direction.

A CEO mentor I had once told me I was overthinking my whole career. He wanted me to be nicer and more chill, so he told me to be more of a dolphin than a shark. Sharks have unfairly earned a bad reputation, while dolphins, who are actually sexual predators, bullies, and sadists (Google it), are widely admired.

This Dolphin CEO told me to be like water with a straight face. His rationale was that he had never applied for a single job in his 30-year career. He just did a good job, and the opportunities flooded in. I explained that that was not my lived experience. I talked to him about double exceptionalism and the pet to threat cycle. I confided that I am still afraid I could be put in my place at any point. His response? I should work on my people skills so that I can be more like water. Whatever the hell that means. I felt I couldn't risk pointing out that I'm pretty good with people already. As usual, it just felt too impolite to point out my own competence, so I just let him believe that I would meditate on it.

I did. Kind of.

What I decided is that immigrant, AuADHD, queer, Black girls do not become executives at huge companies, publish books, and still have the privilege of keeping their ethics because they are *nice* to others. I get that it reads like a humble brag. Still, we really can't survive late-stage capitalism, unemployment, neurotypical violence, or organisational betrayal if we aren't able to set aside politeness to get what we deserve. People confuse my kindness for weakness at their peril, and I genuinely enjoy the look of dread as that particular penny drops. I'm not a dolphin, but I'm also not a shark.

Kindness matters. Respect for others matters. Being nice? Being compliant? Being likeable? Winning? Beating others? To me, that is all amateur hours. But that is just my definition of success. You have my consent to toss that out and pick something else. It doesn't really matter what we pick, but we must pick something that genuinely motivates and fuels us, especially on the bad days. For some, this could be continuous learning; for others, perhaps it's mentoring or volunteering. Whatever it is, let it serve as our yardstick of success and well-being rather than relying on the fickle affirmations of a manager or executive. In environments that attract insecure overachievers, these occasional sparks of recognition are rarely enough to sustain genuine happiness; they're just enough to keep us invested, compliant, and trying to make our Office Dad proud by totally sacrificing our health and sanity. Let's not play ourselves like that.

TRY THIS: DEFINING SUCCESS ON YOUR TERMS

Think about the last time you had a properly great day at work. Not just a day where nothing went wrong, but one where you actually felt brilliant about what you'd accomplished.

Write down what made that day feel successful. Was it because you got loads done? Because you helped someone? Because you learned something that made you think "bloody hell, that's clever"? Was it because you felt useful, or creative, or like you'd actually made a difference?

Now rank those reasons in order of what mattered most to you. Not what should matter, not what your boss would want to matter, but what actually made you feel good.

Look at your top three. Could one of them become your personal definition of success? The thing you measure yourself against when you're lying in bed wondering if you're any good at your job?

Here's the important bit: decide how you'll actually track this. What single thing could you check off each day that would make you think "right, I did well today" regardless of whether anyone else noticed or cared?

Make it something you control completely. Other people's opinions are lovely when they're positive, but they're rubbish as a foundation for feeling accomplished because you never know when they'll change their minds.

Chapter 11

Rewrite Struggles into Stories

A DHD leaders who are in supportive environments are often going to have better outcomes in terms of job satisfaction and longevity in their roles. Many of us, however, do not find ourselves in those supportive environments. In the Neuroinclusion at Work Report 2024, one in three UK organisations admitted that neuroinclusion is not a focus for them. It's not difficult to imagine how challenging it is to get anyone to take ADHDers' challenges and requirements seriously in those organisations. About the same number of organisations (31%) report that their HR, senior leaders, line managers, or employee resource groups talk formally and publicly about neurodiversity (CIPD, 2024).

Having more of a 'career squiggle' than a career path is quite common for ADHDers. Some may have had multiple careers in a short period of time. Someone else might have preferred lateral moves that allowed them to learn across departments (instead of getting more senior in one department). Another person may have moved to a new industry every 18 to 24 months to run away from the boredom of being in their comfort zone for too long. As long as we avoid the temptation to start 'should-ing' ourselves, the squiggle need not be an impediment to getting into a leadership role. It may take longer, but everyone can get there in their own time and in their own way.

One Employer	Company Jumping	Organic Growth
Promotion in same company	*Promotion in new company*	*Go with the flow*
Change Industry	Lateral Moves	Big Risk
Jump to new industry	*Same level on new team*	*Discovery as you go*

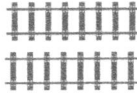

Squiggly career paths

There is something incredibly brave about being able to toss out the rulebook and do whatever we want, but that's not an option for most people. Maybe someone really needs this job and can't afford to make waves. Maybe someone else wants health insurance for their partner and wants to keep their manager happy, or risk losing it. Maybe the person just lost everything in the divorce and needs to start again. Those are situations where one might want to take the shortest and most direct routes to leadership.

TRY THIS: MAPPING YOUR CAREER

Draw a picture of what you thought your career would look like when you started work and what actually happened (i.e., your 'career squiggle'). Where do you first step off the original path and why? How does your path look compared to more traditional paths? What unique perspective or competitive edge has this given you?

> *Now plot key milestones on your career squiggle. These milestones can be significant changes, challenges, or breakthroughs. How has ADHD influenced your career milestones and transitions? What patterns do you notice?*

The other implication is that a potential ADHD leader may be stuck in a corporate environment where a squiggle is almost always a problem for promotion. When I say 'corporate,' I don't necessarily just mean companies that work for profit or private sector organisations. I think of corporates as any place where there are expectations that we show up in a specific uniform, whether that be a suit and tie or an actual uniform, and where we are expected to work primarily in a knowledge worker role rather than a manual worker role. These environments are often, but not always, based in workplaces where most people are interacting with computers, technology, and equipment in ways that use their brains essentially in their jobs. I think these organisations also usually have enough employees that everyone can't be in every meeting. When that happens, we start to introduce things like team meetings, Kanban boards, communications updates, standard operating procedures, or performance metrics by role. In other words, we have to get more corporate.

I also think that an organisation doesn't need to be a for-profit company to be 'corporate.' Even charities develop a kind of respectability politics that employees have to buy into to be successful at a certain size. We can't show up in ripped jeans and a free T-shirt for a job at a charity that has a £100 million annual revenue, right? That is something that does not go down well because it's not the image that the charity wants to portray. It's not the image that a potential leader would want to portray, either. Just as in for-profit workplaces, the rules of engagement are set by unspoken norms and contexts we may know nothing about.

No One Gets Promoted for Being 'Good with People.' Think of Another Strength.

For the love of all things unholy, when someone asks us what our strengths are, please don't say we're good with people. The reason is threefold. First, when people are prompted to describe their strengths, they often default to the generic. Most people haven't spent enough time thinking about what truly constitutes a strength for them. They tend to remember their failures more readily than overlook or underrate their abilities. Being good with people is so vanilla that it seems like it would always be an adequate answer. The reality is that it's like saying our biggest weakness is that we're perfectionists. That may actually be true, but it's a bit of a non-answer. It doesn't offer any insights into what someone is good at or why they should be selected for an opportunity over others. People do need us to be good at something specific to want to work with you.

The second reason is that being good with people is somewhat integral to every job. Ninety-nine per cent of jobs will require us to either understand how people interact in their workplaces or understand people to know how to pretend their behaviour makes sense to you. It's kind of like a make-up artist saying they are good with colours or an accountant saying they are good with numbers. No shit.

The third reason, especially for women, relates to how women are often socialised and perceived. There's a persistent notion that to be likeable, a woman needs to adapt to others' expectations. This is something ingrained from a young age that we don't fully realise the impact it has on our lives and careers, leading us to believe that self-sacrifice is normal and that our role should inherently involve caring for others. This way of thinking is so internalised that we may not even question it as we enter the workplace.

Of course, some men are naturally skilled at interacting with people, and interpersonal skills are more important for certain roles than others. However, I noticed that men described their people skills in different ways. They'd use phrases like 'client rapport', 'influencer', 'team dynamics', or 'understanding people strategy' - corporate terms that don't reduce these skills to 'soft skills'. I'm sceptical of the term 'soft skills' because these interpersonal abilities are arguably among the hardest skills to develop and apply effectively. But I digress.

Professing to be 'good with people' could have weakened my perceived value as a problem solver and analytical thinker, especially in a consulting role where those skills are taken for granted. Additionally, as we advance in our careers, the expectations on the quality of our interpersonal skills change dramatically. Suddenly, we need to manage client relationships, hold senior-level discussions, and establish credibility in rooms where we might be the only woman or have little in common with the decision-makers.

When we introduce ourselves to a new team, it's essential to clearly articulate our skills and the value we'll bring to the project. Instead of saying, 'I'm good with people', or 'I have a positive attitude', consider specifics: 'I'm great at conceptual problem-solving', or 'My written and oral communication skills are exceptional. I have a strong grasp of data analytics. This level of detail allows others to understand where you'll add value to the team. It also gives insight into what we want to develop further and where we see our career heading.

In my case, I enjoy leadership development, mentoring, and coaching, but I do not typically highlight these skills unless specifically asked. I'm not looking for an HR role. There's nothing inherently wrong about being on a people team, but HR is an area where women are overrepresented, often due to stereotypes about their natural care and nurturing abilities. Instead, I focus on my passion for strategic problem-solving, particularly on broader, conceptual issues like organisational culture and market leadership. Highlighting this as one of my strengths positions me for project discussions, which I find more stimulating.

Similarly, I emphasise my communication skills because I know these will be valuable in nearly any project environment. If a manager needs someone to handle a client update, they'll likely delegate it to the person who has shown a talent for communication. However, we must follow through on any strength we declare by proving our credibility early on. This combination of aligning our strengths with team needs and focusing on areas we want to develop shapes how people perceive us.

Ultimately, positioning ourselves is about articulating what we want to be known for and where we're heading in our careers. Avoid getting boxed in by generic phrases like 'good with people' and instead frame our strengths in ways that highlight both our current value and our future potential.

JOURNAL PROMPTS

I adopted the following prompts from an exercise on PositivePsychol ogy.com about exploring strengths and their 'Recognising Your Strengths Worksheet'.

It's a lot easier to list our 'weaknesses' than our strengths. One helpful method to use is thinking about what gives you energy.

In the past week, when did you feel most energised? What strength were you using at the time? Write them down.

Think about the work, side hustle, hobbies, or activities that you enjoy the most. It doesn't matter if you have only done it once or if you're too busy to get to do it often.

> *In what ways do these activities put your strengths to use? In what ways could you use your strengths to find more time/money/energy to do these activities?*

Even Personal Brands Need a Niche

Not many people want to think about personal branding. Depending on how we were raised and how much our cultures valued humility, marketing ourselves can feel arrogant, fake, corporate, or just give you the ick. Regardless, whether we want to or not, every action we take sends a message about who we are to others. We might as well take control of the narrative.

Think of it as cosplay. When we walk into our workplaces, who are we portraying? Maybe we're a charismatic leader who loves high heels and power suits. Or maybe we're a quiet strategist who's always ready with the perfect, random bit of data. Whoever that character is, make it intentional. We can style them however we like, but as long as they align with what we want to be known for.

No, this doesn't mean lying or masking to the point where we're un-recognisable. It just means emphasising the parts of us that align with our strengths while keeping the more personal quirks, especially the ones people might misinterpret, on a need-to-know basis. For example, if someone with ADHD lets their hyperfocus creativity shine, managers might take notice. It's hard to sell yourself based on your weaknesses, so I would not advise that ADHDer to lead with how hard it is to sit through long meetings or how boring they think their current job is. Keep the magic alive, but stay focused on what you bring rather than what you lack.

In MBB consulting, we often spoke about the need for partners to be the best in the world at something, whether that's a niche industry or a specific skill. Some people carve out industry expertise, focusing, say, on banking or pharmaceuticals. Others cultivate functional expertise, like digital transformations, which they can apply across any industry. There are even people who know their client and the people who work there like they're all family. Whatever that special sauce they have is, that's what they become (internally) 'famous' for.

That's a pretty useful way to think about personal brands. Each of us just has to keep asking: 'What do I want to be known for?.' Sometimes the answer is clear. Most of the time, we have no idea.

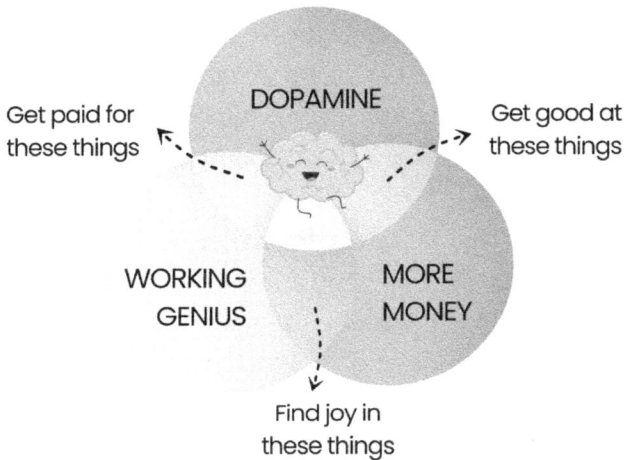

The Venn Diagram of Your Personal Brand

Don't Solve Problems Quietly

When we find complex, high-visibility, high-value topics in our sweet spot, we also need to identify the problems that make these niches important. Once we have confirmed that it matters, we should solve those problems out loud. Not quietly, not efficiently, and not without any fuss. We should aim to solve problems in a way that other people can easily see. That is pretty important.

Unfortunately, our value is very highly correlated with the cost of the problems that we resolve. I think people sometimes confuse avoiding problems with reducing costs. They'll say, 'Ta-da! I did that cool thing so that we didn't have to spend this random amount of money.' They do not realise that cost avoidance isn't perceived the same way as cost reduction. It's not.

Why? Because it's really hard to prove that it would have eventually cost someone some amount if you'd just let the bad outcomes do their thing. It's easy for someone later to say, 'But we don't actually know if it would've happened that way? This person is probably exaggerating. So, avoid hyper-focusing on the kinds of things that will help our companies avoid future costs.

Focus on the kinds of things that remove current costs or, at the very least, give our commercially minded bosses new ways to think that what they're doing is reducing costs. A lot of the time, they will look at headcount or the number of FTEs and say, 'An X% reduction in them is, therefore, an X% reduction in costs'. If we can figure out other ways to show them that we're saving costs through lower utilisation of machinery, lower electricity costs, or lower processing costs, those kinds of things go a long way toward proving that we have executive reasoning capacity.

Successful implementation of this strategy relies on not swooping in to rescue people or situations before the potential problems become actual problems. That might change once we establish a widespread reputation for solving problems. But in the beginning? Let the problem happen. Let the risk materialise before we swoop in with answers or solutions. If we don't do that, then there is no problem to solve, right? We solved something that didn't exist yet; the value of doing that is far less than fixing an actual problem or issue that's occurring in real time. So, deciding when we fix problems is going to be super important.

Here's the key: repetition builds perception. Some people will be sold on us after one interaction, but most will need consistent, varied evidence. They don't need to like us; they just need to know we're excellent at our job. That way, excluding us or ignoring our contributions becomes more of an inconvenience for them than just acknowledging how good we are and letting us get on with that.

As frustrating as it is when people don't know how good we had to be to get where we are, never being able to tell them about it is worse. It seems like being seen as confident is fine, but that is a slippery slope to being arrogant, so we keep cosplaying modesty, making that act part of our brands.

Acknowledging that we're legit good at our jobs is seen as distasteful because we live in a world where people are expected to perform humility constantly. If we don't perform it well enough, it's interpreted as arrogance, ungratefulness, or self-importance. I've never seen anyone ever benefit from being seen as humble, by the way. There does not appear to be an upside beyond feeling like people don't low-key hate you. Leaning into my full AuDHD-ness has made it so much harder to sustain that act. Pretending that I didn't have to be incredibly intelligent, stupidly brave, mercilessly self-aware, and emotionally astute just to get where I am is exhausting.

It's surreal to achieve things that require navigating a minefield of intersecting identities, only to find we're not allowed to acknowledge that stuff was just harder for you. I am expected to minimise the specific barriers I've faced and focus on the silver linings. Neurodiversity has been framed as a superpower by some, but I don't buy into that narrative. Sure, my neurodivergence has given me certain advantages, but to frame it as purely empowering ignores its complexity.

I know some of the factors that shaped me were, frankly, awful. My father running a 'social experiment' on me to turn me into some ruthless, man-destroying, robot CEO was not an ideal upbringing for a sensitive AuDHD kid. In his mind, my future success meant raising me (a Black girl) as though I were an entitled white boy. There were tests, drills, debates, lectures, and manifestos to go along with this social experiment, and it lasted until I left home for university. It made me an expert masker.

Did it make me resilient? Sure. Did I like it? Absolutely not. The narrative that we're supposed to thank every hardship for shaping us into who we are today is a lie. It's okay to say, 'This helped me, but it also hurt me; I wouldn't wish it on anyone else'.

My father's social experiment was also the first time I experienced the 'pet to threat' cycle. He wanted to make me smarter and more ruthless than anyone. He just hadn't bet on me becoming smarter and more ruthless than he was. He eventually disowned me largely because he did not like that he had created something he couldn't control. It only got worse when I learned how much I actually liked being nice to people. Needless to say, he was quite disappointed.

For many fellow 'double exceptional' ADHDers, we live in this constant 'pet to threat' cycle, where, one moment, people are celebrating you, and the next, they're finding ways to push you out for the same things they loved six months ago. Saying that makes people uncomfortable, as though I'm accusing everyone of being complicit. Even though white men have overwhelmingly been the ones who made me both pet and threat, I'm not making a blanket statement about an entire demographic. I'm just pointing out that being the teacher's pet is often a death sentence for your career at that place. People wonder why Black women or ADHDers bounce from one company to another. They think that we are chasing a higher pay cheque when we're just fleeing the scene of our latest character assassination.

Admitting that I am smart doesn't mean I think I'm better than anyone else. It just means I have certain unique cognitive abilities. Yet, acknowledging even that small truth can feel taboo.

People assume I'm being humble when I say 'I'm not the smartest person I know.' But for me, that's just the truth.

Despite all the hard work, the years of struggle, and the incredible rooms I have had access to, there's always the fear that it could all end tomorrow. Someone could take everything away from me just because I challenged the wrong person at the wrong time. When I see the statistics of how many people on the streets are ADHD, Black, queer, immigrants, or disabled, I'm reminded of how luck shaped my life too. I know I've worked hard, but I also know I'm no more deserving than those who didn't have the same breaks.

TRY THIS: ASK FRIENDS ABOUT YOUR PERSONAL BRAND

Ask three or four friends to tell you how you come across in real life and on the internet. Where is the gap between your performance and how they perceive your performance? Ask them how you might close that gap i.e., what would they need to see from you to shift their beliefs positively?

***

TRY THIS: PUTTING YOURSELF OUT THERE

Choose one high-value contribution you typically make behind the scenes. You can decide what 'high-value' means in your context, but things that save or make money are a good start. For one month, make your contribution explicit and visible by trying combinations of:

Offer to do a 'Lunch and Learn' or case study for your team on this thing

Do it but don't share it yet. Wait until someone notices that it hasn't been done. Inform them that you usually do it, but you had to work on other priorities first and forgot to send it on time. Send it immediately.

Document the process/outcome and share it with key stakeholders

---

Teach someone more outgoing and enthusiastic how to do it and rely on them to highlight your expertise

Connect it explicitly to organisational priorities in 1:1 meetings with your boss

Ask your work wife/husband to casually mention your contribution and why it matters in a team meeting

Quantify its impact and include it in a few of your email status updates or contributions to the company's weekly newsletter

Be scientific about it. Track responses and results. Does increased visibility feel uncomfortable but useful, or just uncomfortable? Did people change the way they viewed you after knowing the work you were doing behind the scenes? Test and iterate ways that feel authentic for you to get the credit that you earned.

Chapter 12

Lead With Your Genius

M y proudest professional achievement remains the six months I spent in Sierra Leone supporting the establishment of a presidential delivery unit to implement the country's Ebola recovery plan. In 2015, I arrived just after the peak of the Ebola crisis, but the virus was still raging. All schools were closed for a year, and I was tasked with an enormous challenge: working alone, without a supporting team, manager, or partner. I was literally dropped off at the Ministry of Education, Science, and Technology with the directive to 'get 1.8 million children back in school safely.'

'Good luck,' said the project manager before driving away, leaving me there.

It became an inspiring experience as I joined a ministry team working with various private, civil society, and public sector partners. We developed the first curriculum in 20 years, implemented a national school feeding programme, built hundreds of new schools, and conducted the first country-wide teacher training in over two decades. We built an alternative education system for pregnant teenagers banned from school.

The same project also represents my greatest failure. During those months in Sierra Leone, I completely ignored everyone's advice, including my body's signals. I worked seven days a week because everyone else was putting in 14 to 16-hour days. I drank heavily to cope with the stress of living through a pandemic and being separated from family for months (I'd signed a waiver with South Africa's Health Department agreeing they could deny me re-entry if I contracted Ebola).

The pressure was immense, but my approach was worse. I harboured this attitude that I knew best, genuinely cared about this country, and despite not being the most qualified or intelligent person, it was my responsibility to do everything possible, even at the cost of my own health, to make this work.

By month five, I experienced a full psychotic break because no one told me you couldn't take malaria tablets for six months. I lost the ability to distinguish between dreams and reality. I became convinced someone was stealing money from my hotel room, though the amounts were oddly specific: $200 would become $180, then $120 the next day. This thief was inexplicably leaving me the change.

In an uncharacteristic 'Karen' moment, I exploded at the head of security, demanding to know who had accessed my room. He apologised profusely, then printed records showing that only I had entered my room for the past two weeks. When I asked how he explained the missing money, he simply said, 'Ma'am, I can't explain this besides spirits. Ghosts.' Remarkably, in my impaired mental state, I responded, 'Okay, but can we please tell the people who work here to tell the ghost to stop stealing from me?' before walking back to my room.

The whole situation was far more difficult than necessary because I had fallen for the seductive, luxurious idea of the hardcore consultant lifestyle while simultaneously playing the role of a performatively liberal,

warm-hearted crusader for African peoples. I hadn't recognised the sav-
iour complex I'd developed as a consultant.

Fixing this failure took a long time, and initially, I tried all the wrong
approaches. I worked even harder. I sought more mentors, sponsors,
and coaches, even when I didn't need them or understand why I had
them. I was desperately gathering people to support and take an interest
in me, but it rarely worked because I was spreading myself too thin.

Eventually, recovery required changing nearly everything in my life. I
changed the types of projects I took on and the partners I worked with.
I adjusted my expectations of what constituted a good workday, from
16 hours down to 12 (still not healthy, but progress). I improved my
nutrition, drank less, and exercised more. I found a therapist and began
discussing workplace challenges and their emotional impact.

When people ask what I learned from working myself into psychosis, I
often talk about the importance of teams or the principle that we should
never care more about a project than the client does, adding my own
twist that we should never care more about the project or the client than
we care about ourselves.

These sound like wonderful LinkedIn-ready insights, but the real lesson was humbling. I'm just not that smart. I genuinely believed I could
single-handedly transform Sierra Leone's education system. The reality
is that I was stumbling through like everyone else, doing my best in difficult circumstances. But 'my best' wasn't truly my best because a better
approach would have involved seeking help, collaborating with partners
on problem-solving, working more closely with clients, and maintaining
proper records of my work.

What would have helped? Asking anyone for help. I admit that I needed
help. Asking others to delegate less to me. We see the trend, I hope.
Leadership is a team sport. No one is smart enough to do it alone.

All of this taught me that I'm neither as smart nor as competent as I thought. I absolutely need people alongside me who can support me, challenge me, and tell me to stop working at 22:00. I wish I'd learned these lessons before working myself until I couldn't walk on one leg during one project or until my body seized up on another, requiring emergency muscle relaxants just so I could stand upright. I wish I hadn't worked through fevers or almost dying from bilharzia. I wish I hadn't repeatedly burned out so completely that I needed solitary holidays just to sleep for five days straight.

I consider all of these massive failures, though they often read as successes because the projects turned out so well. I did a great job by most measures. The clients loved the work and thought it was amazing, but inside, I was crumbling. That failure taught me a vital lesson on my leadership journey, one I'm grateful for because it ensures I'll never feel that way again. Don't go it alone.

Are You the Problem?

There is certainly some benefit in not over-personalising what's hap-pening to your employees and making it all about you because I've certainly also been that person trying to be the martyr and destroy my own career for the sake of people more junior to me. Honestly, that didn't serve them or me in any particular way. It just made me feel a bit morally smug and good about myself. I was doing the right thing in very heavy inverted commas, but they didn't really benefit from my moral high ground. The people who worked for me were much better served by diplomacy, by increasing my understanding and curiosity about other people, by learning the dynamics on different teams.

I once had a boss who worked out that one of our clients was incredibly racist, sexist, and pretty much refused to work with me. My boss was an Italian, prone to spontaneous celebration and passionate displays (let's call him Pizza). One ordinary Tuesday, the racist client exposed his bias in a meeting with my boss, Pizza. I expected Pizza to ignore it as most of my South African bosses would have done. Instead, he stopped a meeting, stood up and shouting at this guy, basically told him, 'If you ever speak to her again that way, if you ever show any signs of your own bias like this again, this entire time will leave you and this building immediately.'

We can argue about whether that's a strong enough deterrent. We are the consultants so the power should be in favour of the client. At this particular telco though, the programme we worked on was literally on fire and they had people calling each other bitches in exec meetings. They need some serious intervention. It's not really the kind of thing that you can solve internally, especially when you're running two years over and double budget on one of your most important projects. So, Pizza's threat was very credible.

This guy had some fairly overt tactics, including fully ignoring me in meetings, sending emails to everyone besides me, and the usual mayonnaise version of discrimination. What is interesting is that he also suffered from being bad at his job.

This is something which I learned very early on about leadership and about managers specifically. You can get away with being a jerk at a high-performing company as long as you perform more impressively than you piss people off.

If your value exceeds the opportunity cost of retaining better talent, then all good. The challenge is if you're only average at your job, but you are heavy on the problems. You become a liability to your bosses, and it becomes very easy for them to suddenly care very much about toxic workplace behaviour and get rid of you.

For those who are bad at their jobs, the reason they're getting fired may have little to do with their toxic behaviour, but that toxicity does provide a convenient rationale for getting rid of some dead weight.

Pizza never confirmed or denied it but, two weeks later, the client was mysteriously leaving the company. I believe he moved to Australia and one of Pizza's allies took his place.

Honestly, I'm not sure whether I think that is the right or the wrong way to approach these things. The question is not should people who are bad at their jobs and racist be celebrated. The real question is whether people who are great at their jobs and racist should be tolerated. In theory, absolutely not. In practice? Employment matters are a little bit more complicated in real life.

It's also possible for someone to be an ally and also very much not be an ally in different parts of their lives. Like an exec who once told me that I needed to stop changing my hairstyle because no one would be able to tell me apart from any of the other Black women in the office... who all looked very distinctly different from me. I don't think he was trying to be racist. I think he was just accidentally racist in trying to be an ally for my career and workplace visibility.

That's why, regardless of whether we think we're part of the problems or the solutions, we should still take the time to check.

Start with: How would I feel if someone was saying this to me? Would I be comfortable for my children and my friends and my chosen religious leader to know that I had said this to another person? Would I be embarrassed if this came out in the newspapers tomorrow?

All of those are pretty good checks for bosses in particular to ask themselves frequently about whether the nature of what they're saying is really worth the risk or hurt that they are creating.

Genuine mistakes do happen. Managers are just people and people aren't just one thing at a time. They're a layer of fears, motivations, insecurities, strengths, weaknesses, principles, ethics, all at once, and those operate differently depending on which context they're in. Sadly, leaders aren't yet human brains aren't 'if-then' machines. We aren't programmed in a way to make entirely logical choices every time.

My own weaknesses and bias as a leader inform a lot of my choices on recruiting, staffing, and building teams. I look for people who are allies where I am an outsider. They need to have what I don't and have 50/50 vision where I have blind spots. That especially includes people who make more logical choices than I do at times. I've tried many approaches for hacking this selection process. Working Genius is my current tool of choice.

Working Genius and Building a Team That Actually Leads Together

Putting together teams that work together is tough, especially when you are creating teams with more neurodifferent than most. Knowing what people are most capable of and where in the team they would be most valuable often takes a long time, repeated exposure, and juggling what people like doing and what you need them to do. For ADHDers, their capacity and capability are consistently inconsistent.

Even with similar profiles, skills, and tenure, one ADHDer can smash out a project plan in thirty minutes, whilst another would rather stab themselves with a fork than make a Gantt chart in Excel. The Working

Genius model helped me make sense of these differences in preference and productivity and staff teams accordingly.

I first came across Patrick Lencioni's Working Genius framework when I was trying to figure out why some team members could not be coached on important topics, despite really wanting to learn and being pretty smart. It's one of those models that once you understand it, you can't unsee the patterns in your team.

The WIDGET Framework

Lencioni identifies six types of 'working genius' that work in pairs, and we can remember them with the acronym WIDGET. Each of us has two areas of 'genius' (things we're both good at and enjoy), two 'competencies' (things we can do but don't love), and two 'frustrations' (things that drain our will to live). WIDGET stands for:

- W is for Wonder - These people are perpetually curious, always asking 'What if?' and 'Could this be better?' They spot problems and opportunities that others miss.

- I is for Invention - These folks love creating solutions from scratch. Give them a blank page and they'll fill it with brilliant ideas. They're happiest when innovating without constraints.

- D is for Discernment - These are the people who evaluate ideas quickly and ruthlessly. They'll tell you which of your seventeen solutions might actually work and why the others are rubbish. They will probably be right.

- G is for Galvanising - These are the rally-the-troop types who get everyone excited about an idea. Think of them as the politicians of the workplace – love hyping up a team, brilliant at getting buy-in and getting people ready to go... but not necessarily doing the work themselves.

- E is for Enabling - These are the helpers who ask, 'How can I support you with this?' They're brilliant at making things happen for others and filling in the gaps. I call them the bureaucrats who take what the politicians promise and make it real for everyone else.

- T is for Tenacity - These are the finishers who power through to completion. They love ticking items off a list and ensuring everything gets done properly.

Remember when I said everyone has two of these WIDGET letters as their working genius, two are their working competence, and two as their frustrations? Our working genius is where we will add the most value, shine brightest, and have the most fun. We are okay at our competencies, but they aren't our favourite things to do. Our frustrations are the things we would rather face a stabbing fork from the previous page than deal with. Let's talk about mine as a practical example.

WONDER
The Dreamer

Craves: Being worthy of consideration

Avoids: Uncurious people

IDEATE
The Inventor

Craves: Making new ideas and things with no limits

Avoids: Constraints, copying

DISCERN
The Judge

Craves: Others trust their judgement implicitly

Avoids: Demands to "Prove it"

GALVANISE
The Politician

Craves: Their words trigger reactions and progress

Avoids: Apathy

ENABLE
The Helper

Craves: Simple appreciation

Avoids: Being ignored, underappreciated, or overlooked

TENACITY
The Closer

Craves: Clarity and permission to do what needs to be done

Avoids: Ambigiuity, tweaks

Six Types of Working Genius

My genius pairing is Ideation and Discernment, making me what Lencioni and team would call 'an ID.' I love coming up with ideas and frameworks, even when that wasn't really the assignment. I'm also quite good at independently evaluating which ideas are crap and which might actually be worth pursuing. It's why when I present an idea, I've usually already thought through the obvious objections. My competencies are W and E. I can be curious about the big picture, and I can help others, but these activities don't fill me with excitement. I've had male colleagues constantly push me toward enabling because I'm a woman. They assume that's where I'll be most comfortable and useful. But being forced to operate in the frustration zone is soul-destroying if it's required frequently enough. It doesn't just make for less effective employees; it literally sucks out their will to live.

I had a male friend who was a natural Enabler (E). After learning about Working Genius, he literally hugged me with tears in his eyes because he finally understood why he always felt inadequate in corporate settings. He loved helping others succeed, but that's often interpreted as a weakness in business. The real weakness is forcing people to work against their natural strengths.

My frustrations are G and T. I absolutely loathe having to stand in front of people trying to get them excited about something. I can do it for about thirty minutes before I want to lie down in a dark room for three hours. And if you give me a detailed list of tasks to complete in sequence without deviation, I will find twenty reasons why I forgot the list existed after about two minutes. I tell myself that I need to follow my energy and interests, not a rigid plan, but in reality, lists just bore me. There is no invention required, and my joy is in making things up, not getting things done.

Lencioni says, 'No joy, no genius.' That's the key insight. Genius is not just about what we're good at. It's also about what gives us energy rather than draining it. When I'm working in my genius areas, I have incredible resilience. If people reject my ideas, I'll happily generate more. But if I'm trying to galvanise a room full of blank-faced executives, I'm mentally planning my escape route within minutes.

Imbalance Destroys Teams

This model explains so much about teams that just can't get anything done. I once worked with an executive team composed almost entirely of Galvanisers and Tenacity types (GTs). These are the 'always be closing' people who are constantly rallying the troops, pushing for sales, or getting mad because people aren't hyped enough.

They'd spend all day sending motivational/threatening emails and setting impossible targets. Then they'd be utterly baffled when nothing got done. Why? Because there was no one helping people actually do the work (no Enablers), and no one evaluating which ideas were worth pursuing (no Discernment). They also had terrible ideas for making more money (no Ideation). They were basically a bunch of cheerleaders with no players on the field.

This GT dominance is surprisingly common in leaders. There's this assumption that as you climb the ladder, you can stop being an Enabler or having Tenacity because those are 'junior' roles. You just need to have big ideas (Wonder) and evaluate them (Discernment). But without a balanced team, you get chaos.

I once tried explaining this to a GT CEO who kept coming up with random new initiatives every morning. One day, it was 'We need to build an AI bot!' The next week, it was 'AI is bad for our bottom line, so no more bots!.' When I suggested this constant flip-flopping might not be the best use of company resources, he looked at me like I'd suggested we all work in our underwear. His lack of discernment meant the whole organisation was constantly chasing shiny new things rather than products and services that grew the business.

Using Working Genius in Your Team

Once I understood this model, it transformed how I built teams and assigned work.

At the Firm, we were rewarded for coming up with great ideas or being able to challenge the ideas of others. Brainstorming was just part of the toolkit that everyone had, and I transferred that belief in ideation as a foundational skill to my corporate roles. I spent a lot of time asking my G-E team member to come up with ideas from scratch as a development opportunity. Once I realised that ID was her frustration, we switched to having me solve a problem quickly and hand it over to her to implement, systemise, and promote it; something she genuinely enjoyed.

I work best with the freedom to do things my way. Open-ended exploratory briefs energise me, I hate being told what to do, and I assumed everyone was like that. Working genius showed me that my WT-type team member needed crystal-clear instructions with defined boundaries. Without that specificity, he just went into an anxiety spiral where he started questioning if we were even working on the right problem to begin with (embracing his W like a safety blanket because I couldn't just tell him what I wanted).

I started deliberately hiring balanced teams. Where I didn't have the right mix of all six types, I borrowed people and peers from other teams to help us compensate for our lack of genius in that area.

Filling out a team map of our geniuses as a group has helped me get better at knowing who to slot where and how to keep everyone energised doing what they are best at.

JOURNAL PROMPTS

> *1. Without overthinking it, which two WIDGET types instantly resonat-ed with you? Which two made you think, "Please no, anything but that"?*
>
> *2. What percentage of your current role requires you to operate in your frustration zones? What's one thing you could delegate or restruc-ture to reduce this?*
>
> *3. Who on your current team complements your frustrations with their genius? Who might be struggling because their genius isn't being utilised?*
>
> *4. Which senior leader could be your ally in creating more space for your Working Genius to shine at work?*

Understanding our working genius profile doesn't just help bosses build better teams – it helps us build better careers. If we're constantly exhausted and demoralised at work, we might be operating too much in our frustration zones.

For me, discovering I was an ID explained why I love creating frame-works and writing books, but I get super stressed when I have to im-plement detailed plans that require getting people excited about doing the work. It's why I thrive in roles that let me solve novel problems but struggle in highly regimented environments.

An unexpected benefit to this knowledge was that I stopped feeling guilty about not enjoying certain tasks. It wasn't laziness, incompetence, or even ADHD that caused that task paralysis. I was just working against my genius, which made the problem about how to get it done rather than why I couldn't do it.

I stopped trying to fix my frustrations and think this is a fast track to happier jobs for ADHDers in particular. Instead of working on weakness-es that I will never get better at, I suggest we build teams that comple-ment us and find roles that play to our genius. Our path to leadership isn't about becoming well-rounded if you subscribe to this model. It's about becoming so brilliant in your areas of genius that people forgive you for being rubbish at the rest. What could be more ADHD than that?

Chapter 13
Find Allies to Trust

Remember when everyone with satellite television or a certain streaming service was obsessed with Game of Thrones? Other generations of American TV watchers had Friends or Seinfeld. My generation had Game of Thrones as its weekly must-watch cultural ritual. Retrospectively, I'm embarrassed about how much I loved that show, given its extreme hatred of women and pointless sexual violence, but I digress...

The show was deliciously dark, featuring scheming, backstabbing, political genius, and extreme levels of pettiness. If you're too young to remember Game of Thrones, then think of it as Squid Game. The principle is the same. Corporate environments become more like those surreal TV shows the higher we rise in seniority. Not everyone is Machiavelli, but I don't know any executive who hasn't had to play some Game of Thrones-style mind games at some point. They weren't necessarily villains, but a good number of them probably were.

If we want to win this kind of game, we need to know who's important and who isn't. This is really tough for the neurodivergent brain because we often have an innate sense of equity and justice. It really matters to us that people are treated fairly and equitably, largely because of our own experiences of marginalisation. It would feel strange, even wrong, to look at someone, judge their value, and decide they're not worth the effort of interacting with or developing. We understand how those snap judgments can reverberate and impact the rest of someone's life. So, yes, this one is a hard pill to swallow.

In any office environment, there are always people who are more or less important. I believe this principle applies to any workplace. To be fair, though, I have less experience working as a professional athlete, in a factory, in a retail store, or out in a field growing crops, so I'll confine myself to talking about offices. Sometimes, who matters isn't even determined by the hierarchy or organisational structure. Those are just lines and boxes. There will always be influential people who have the ears of leaders who advise those higher up. We know the type, the ones who, when they speak, everyone else goes quiet, even if they're speaking softly. They don't have to fight for their voice to be heard. Or, when there's a discussion happening, the leader asks for their opinion, their take, or what they think, showing that it's valued above others.

Those are the key people. We need to figure out their problems and how to help solve them. No, we don't have to suck up to them or ingratiate ourselves in some weird, subservient way. What we need to understand is: What do they want? What do they need? What is their problem? Can we match any of those things with our expertise, relationships, or experience? If we can, then we become valuable to them.

Now, let's talk about the ones who technically hold a high rank or position, but nobody respects them. We know, the executives everyone on the board secretly hates, the ones whose ideas are met with thinly veiled snickers or outright indifference. We don't need to treat those people poorly (never do that), but we also don't need to make them our mentors or sponsors. That's not going to help you. We need political capital; those folks aren't going to give it to you.

Instead, we focus our efforts on the calculated relationships that matter. Get on the radar of the key players. Volunteer for initiatives that interest them. Maybe they're organising a charity offsite for the team, offer to help. Do something aligned with what they care about. However, remember that it must be about what they want, not what we think they want. Test assumptions by talking to others who know them or with a little (legal) Google stalking.

The 'important' people influence promotions. They will either do so directly by making the decisions themselves or indirectly because they're on the committee or influence it in some other way. We need to know who is on those committees, how they operate, and what they value. They are in the room where it happens.

If we have no clue how people get into leadership roles in our organisation, we should talk to the leaders. Ask them about the process, how things work. This might require us to feign a little extra enthusiasm for their wisdom than we actually feel. But it's not a lie: we genuinely need that information. Don't waste your energy on people who don't influence those processes.

This probably sounds like playing politics. We all hate office politics. Unfortunately, if we're going to be the boss, we're going to need to suck it up and get good at politics. Politics are unavoidable. Every hierarchical organisation is political. Period. We can't avoid it, so stop trying. Instead, understand how alliances work. Figure out who's aligned with whom on what lines. Even political rivals will find common ground on certain issues. We need to identify those shared priorities because those topics will likely be winners, regardless of who is managing or leading.

While I certainly understand the frustration with politics in organisations, I do not believe that managers get to opt out of politics. In fact, I think they have no option but to engage in politics to win. The reasons for doing this have nothing to do with promoting their own careers and everything to do with what is required to provide air cover for their teams.

Power Hungry or Protecting Others?

The unspoken rules of leadership may emphasise the importance of achieving power and growing our team so that we can get 'leverage.' In this context, power is about getting more done. It's about being able to democratise that power across our team with delegation. It may mean that a bigger team is not necessarily the best option. What we want is a high-performing team that allows us to delegate effectively.

The idea of our boss trying to democratise/delegate power in the hopes of creating leverage may feel a little bit awkward when we are an emerging neurodivergent leader. Neurodivergent team members often have no interest in being anyone's proxies or are less likely to view authority as a badge of honour. They may only care about getting the work done. Being the temporary boss could feel more like a burden than a boon. That is a problem if we see it in the neurodivergent way, but our boss inconveniently needs us to be their delegate or proxy to borrow their authority so we can do things like take holidays.

One helpful way to get around this is reframing. If the mental sound-track isn't serving you, change it. Once we have switched to a new track, power is no longer important because it makes us better than others. Instead, power is important because it gives us the ability to think for ourselves. We earn self-determination and trust when we have power. Even if we're not making the decisions ourselves, we still get a say in what those decisions are. Getting some freedom without the risk is a very different proposition for an emerging neurodivergent leader. There are more advantages to consider. If we have sufficient political capital, we can champion our team's innovation and lend them some political capital when they hit road bumps. If they mess up, they can get another chance because we have enough credibility to be trusted to turn things around without needing to fire people.

That kind of protection is particularly important for neurodivergent employees because there will often be mavericks who think of things in a completely different way and may not always express those things in a way that is acceptable in the corporate culture. They may not express themselves in ways that make them sound like they're team players, regardless of the fact that they really do want to do a good job for the most part.

Having that political capital is essentially having some money in the bank that we are saving for their potential rainy days. It is important to have a positive balance of credibility in the organisation so that when a team member does something that inevitably shakes their credibility, we can intervene. It's obvious but still worth saying: we cannot protect our team if we don't have the power to do that. That's why I think it's not a bad thing to accumulate power intentionally. We are constantly burning through it to support our team members. We are essentially carb-loading. There is a marathon ahead, and that marathon requires us to be fuelled. It is not about eating for the sake of eating. That is why we should look for opportunities to be the delegate/proxy and lean into playing this mini-office version of Game of Thrones.

We will need allies to win this game. That means we need to figure out which of our peers we can trust. Spoiler Alert: We cannot trust all of them. Some people will happily cheer us on as we climb the ladder, only to cut our Achilles tendon at the top with gossip or sabotage, watching us tumble so they can use our downfall as their next step up.

How Do We Figure Out Who to Trust? The Trust Equation

Start by selectively sharing information. If we've only told one person about our interest in a project, and suddenly, everyone knows, they are not trustworthy. Even if they shared it with good intentions, it's still a breach unless we're strategically planting information. That's not someone we should trust.

This is where understanding the difference between work relation-ships and home relationships becomes crucial. Home relationships are with people we've invited into our lives outside work. You've been to each other's homes, not for work purposes but to socialise genuinely. Those are our real friends. Work friends? They're friendships of convenience. We hang out during work hours, maybe grab lunch together or join team events. But if that's the extent of it, they're not real friends. They're like a Monday-to-Friday friendship, and that's fine, but don't mistake it for a true bond. Keep your guard up.

Just because someone is a 'home friend' doesn't mean we owe them advocacy in the workplace, especially if they're not advocating for them-selves. Yes, it feels good to support someone and do the right thing, but let's be honest – it's not always the smartest move for our career. If this person is an adult with the agency, let them advocate for themselves or at least ask us to do it explicitly. Otherwise, we're just sticking our neck out for someone who might not even realise, or appreciate, that we're doing it. If there's no clear incentive for us beyond warm, fuzzy feelings, think twice. The trust equation is a great tool to understand the components of trust in an ND-friendly way. The equation suggests that if you want someone to trust you in any capacity, but especially professionally, the formula is:

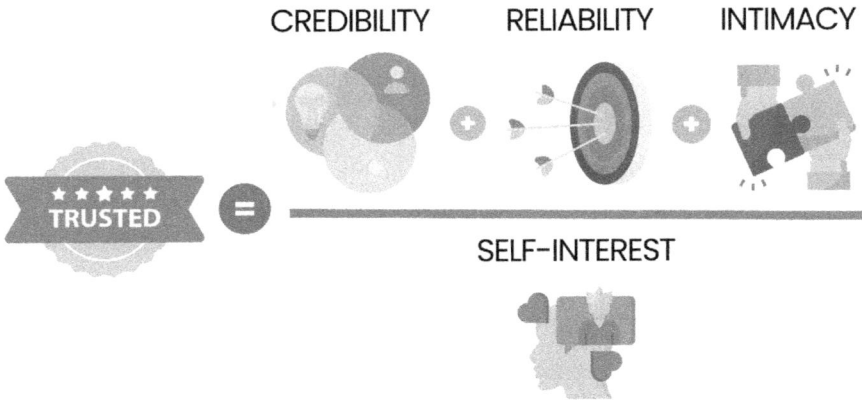

The Trust Equation

Trust = (Credibility + Reliability + Intimacy) ÷ Self-orientation. Let's break down each component of the formula:

Credibility

This means they know that you know what you're talking about. Credibility can come from several sources:

- Content expertise (specific knowledge of methodologies or technologies)

- Relationship expertise (understanding the organisation and its people)

- Reasoning ability (capacity to work through complex problems)

- Reputation (track record and brand within the industry)

I personally 'sell' myself on content and subject-matter knowledge because I like knowing what I'm talking about and find that easier than random small talk. But that means I need to go into sessions with someone who knows the industry, has relationships, and has a great reputation to fill the gaps in my credibility.

I personally lead with content expertise because I'm most confident discussing transformation frameworks and approaches. But this means I need team members who bring the other elements, particularly those with strong existing relationships in the organisation

Reliability

This means when you say you'll do something, you do it. This includes:
Arriving on time
Being prepared
Following through on commitments
Not requiring reminders or constant checking

Reliability with your team translates directly to reliability with clients. For my direct reports, I choose team members who consistently deliver and arrive prepared. Nothing undermines an executive relationship faster than missed deadlines or half-baked deliverables.

Intimacy

This means you care about them as a human and have a closeness to them. Not everyone can make others instantly like them. I'm an introvert, so I often choose to work with extroverts who can strike up conversations and make small talk. Building rapport based on who you are rather than attempting to be someone else is crucial. I lean into authenticity as a way to build intimacy with people. Understanding your own personality and strengths helps you build rapport authentically.

For intimacy, I recognise my limitations as an introvert. I often include more extroverted team members who naturally build rapport through small talk and personal connections. This balances my more direct, content-focused approach.

Self-orientation

This is the denominator in the equation because the more self-interested you are, the less trustworthy you are as soon as clients can see that what you're trying to do is to suit your own purposes, that immediately reduces the amount of trust they have for you.

Low self-orientation means:

- Focusing on the client, not yourself

- Making them the hero, not you

- Caring about their outcomes more than your own

- Listening more than speaking

- Being honest about whether your solution is right for them

The lower your self-orientation, the higher the trust.

Chapter 14

Sponsorship Isn't Just for Conferences

To thrive in the corporate cult, we need a sponsor. Sponsors take risks for those they sponsor, using their political capital to advocate for them and provide cover when mistakes inevitably occur. A sponsor is someone with the authority to help us advance, even when we've made mistakes. I've been lucky to have sponsors who've had my back when things went wrong. Finding a sponsor is a game-changer. Mentors, coaches, and teachers were great, but sponsors are the ones who really made my career. A significant body of research also suggests that this is true for many women in many organisations. The make-or-break for them tends to come down to sponsors.

Most organisations, however, do not have the language of consulting. They only have 'sponsors' for projects, not dedicated people. So, I'll briefly explain what I mean when I say this: that we start from the same base. A sponsor is easiest explained by talking about what it is not first. A mentor is someone who provides us with information and advice based on their personal experience. Several studies have found that mentors play a critical role in helping ADHDers navigate workplace challenges and build resilience (Garber, 2001). A coach is someone who asks you question until you arrive at your own answers; they provide clarity through the process of allowing you to work things out yourself. A teacher will tell you the things that they have learned, not necessarily things that they have done or learned from real-world practice. A sponsor is the person who buys you credibility through their endorsement.

The explanation I use to make this real is one that I 100 per cent stole from Joanna Barch, a former senior partner at McKinsey & Company who wrote an incredible book about leadership: *'How Remarkable Women Lead'*. Barsh uses an analogy that starts with someone we like or love asking us to go skydiving. We have a brief lapse of good sense and agree. When we arrive at the skydiving place, we have a one-on-one kind of theoretical lecture. During that, they will tell us what to expect. They tell us what to look out for and what's challenging. That's the teacher. We then move on to the person who is going to help suit us up and talk us through what's going to happen. They're going to make sure that we've put things on correctly. That person is giving us that information based on their experience because they're usually the instructor, the person with whom we might be doing the jump.

There will then be, of course, a time when they are asking us some questions to make sure that we understand, to help us work out where our gaps are, to allay any fears, et cetera. They're prompting us based on information they know, information that we will need to make sure that we have the best. That is the coaching aspect. We can see it's slightly different from the mentoring that they did when they were showing us practically how to do something, because one was from their own experience, and the second was using their experience to ask the right questions. We then get to the sponsor, the person who is with us once we are up in the air in the plane. There is a pilot, and there is someone whose job it is to push us out of the plane. Obviously, consensually, but a lot of times, people need someone who is either going to push them out or who's going to jump in tandem with them, such that they are able to achieve a goal that they've set themselves, regardless of their fear in the moment. That person who's either pushing us out of the plane or jumping out of it with us is our sponsor.

They are someone who's putting their reputation on the line for yours. They're lending you their political capital credibility so you can build yours. There is a risk involved in them doing this, as shown in the example. The person teaching us in the room, the person helping us put on our gear, and the person asking us the final questions are all on the ground. They don't actually need to get up on the plane with you. The only person who has to do that is the sponsor. That example, I think, also shows why it's so important to have sponsors because, of course, we can do that without anybody around. You *could* do your first skydiving jump having no one push you or jump in tandem, but it's not *recommended* because if something goes wrong, you would have no clue how to salvage the situation. Maybe you pull the cord wrong, maybe you have some kind of episode - the exact disaster obviously doesn't matter. For someone inexperienced in skydiving, any variation from the norm is incredibly dangerous. I think the same is true for trying to become an executive or senior manager in the corporate world. It is an environment that is very unforgiving of mistakes, especially for women or minority groups. I often talk about how women are promoted based on perfection, while men are promoted based on potential. This is a great example of this because, in some sense, men can afford to not be excellent at all times; that's never going to be seen as a reflection of all men. The same goes for ADHD and non-ADHD professionals.

Imagine a non-ADHDer who previously messed up spectacularly in a particular senior role. In that case, that's not going to be used against or considered a factor to be aware of with all future non-ADHDers. If an ADHDer messes up, everyone with ADHD becomes a riskier proposition for line managers.

TRY THIS: PLANNING HOW TO BUILD POLITICAL CAPITAL

Political capital isn't just accumulated passively. Create a deliberate strategy to build it by identifying:

- *Three ways you could visibly solve problems that matter to key leaders*

- *Two alliances you could strengthen with influential colleagues*

- *One area where you could become a recognised expert*

Choose one action from each category to implement this month. Track changes in how your ideas are received or how often you're included in important conversations.

I remember in my early days in consulting, trying to get promoted ahead of schedule simply because I felt like I was really ready; it wasn't the sort of environment where there were only a certain number of places for more senior people. So, we got promoted when we were ready. One of my sponsors very rationally explained to me that, in the past, they had given Black women promotions in their minds too early or really at the cusp of them being ready. This often resulted in them not being able to progress any further because they'd been promoted too early and were not able to meet the requirements of the next level. So, they talked about giving Black women more runway, which meant promoting them later than their peers, such that when they got promoted, they were more than adequately ready for the role that they were stepping into. Thus, they could manage to progress and become a partner at the same time as their peers.

Now, this is problematic for a number of reasons. One, because the idea of giving Black women 'runway' is basically giving them more time to be bad at something simply because they are Black women. That is incredibly awkward.

It is also problematic because my potential was decided on the basis of other women whom I had never met and never interacted with; our only shared characteristics were our ethnicity and gender. That is incredibly challenging because there's no way that we can argue for someone else's case or against someone else's case when we do not know of it; it happened years before you'd even joined that company.

I was incredibly upset by this and was able to convince my sponsors that this was, in fact, rather problematic. They thought it was altruistic to give me that extra time; it was an awkward conversation to explain why it really wasn't. I wouldn't have even been able to have that conversation if I hadn't had a sponsor at all because no one would've told me that information, in part because some of them would never have experienced it individually. They might know of someone who has experienced it, but not necessarily have first-hand knowledge of it. Someone who is *not* our sponsor has no incentive to be honest with us at that level, simply because that is hurtful information to have. Still, it's also dangerous information to have because it's the kind of thing we can then use against our employer to talk about unfair dismissal, get some form of employee tribunal or a settlement agreement out of it.

So, it is not something that someone can just randomly tell you. Likely, they are trusting you to treat this information as for-your-eyes-only intel in your arsenal to turn a situation around or put it to your advantage in a pinch. They're giving you this un-PC information as a reassurance that it's nothing personal.

Our confidence should not be knocked by the fact that we haven't been promoted because it's not really about *us*. It's about a legacy that's created by perceptions that people had about completely separate human beings. I was really grateful to have those sponsors, especially since at the beginning of my career, I was not actively cultivating sponsors. I think that many of the people who were my first sponsors always started as mentors and sometimes as managers. They began to want to give back the same amount that I was giving to their projects, which was often going above and beyond.

I was often the person who was working on client proposals long before I was in any kind of management position, not just because I found them super interesting but also because I recognised that a lot of sponsors are not sponsors out of the goodness of their hearts, unfortunately. Many sponsors are motivated by the belief that their support will yield a return. That return may not necessarily be financial. It could be political. It could be just the feeling of having more leverage to do a great job. It could be the pride in having mentored someone who has a particular talent. There are multiple things, but it is unlikely that they're doing it with no expectation of something in return. We may not be the person giving them what they are getting in exchange. It could be some reward or incentive that they're getting from an external place.

So, for example, in some places of work, mentoring, coaching, and sponsoring are part of our job description. It is not an extra thing that we're doing to someone. It's not a favour that we're doing them. I recall being at The Firm and needing to fill out a form that talked about who my sponsors were and who I was sponsoring. Interestingly, if I had put down someone whom I thought was sponsoring me, who then did not put me down as someone they were sponsoring, that became a problem; it was flagged to that person because they'd created the impression that they were supporting me when they really weren't.

This happened to a Black female partner at the time who was informed that I had put her down as a sponsor. She had not put me down as someone she was sponsoring. To her credit, she really did step up. She was like, 'Okay, that was unexpected but I'm going to get you in front of clients. I'm going to give you opportunities to speak at meetings. I'm going to take you with me when I go to see the president." She delivered on all of those suggestions. I recognised that, on the one hand, it was her job as a partner. She didn't really have a choice about sponsoring people. But I also know that she didn't necessarily have to sponsor *me*. She could have just corrected my assumption and informed me that while she was happy to be a mentor to me or a coach to me, she didn't have the capacity for sponsorship. Instead, she decided to take a different route. I was able to help her get more stuff done, so there was kind of a win in it for her, too.

We don't have to have one mentor, one coach, or one sponsor. We can have multiple. In fact, those people change over time. I had a mentor whose only notable quality to me was her ability to balance her home and work life. She had multiple children, was happily married, and was still performing at a very high level in that organisation. I was married without children, but I certainly found it incredibly difficult to sustain a meaningful, intimate relationship with the demands of a job that took 16 to 18 hours a day every day.

Once I felt that I had addressed that disparity and had found time not just for my relationship but also to do things that I really enjoyed, like writing naturally, that relationship from a mentoring perspective ended. I no longer felt the need to draw on her experiences or seek counsel in that sense. Neither of us was upset about it because she had helped me immensely. I was really grateful for that, but I then needed other help. For example, I was really interested in how I could express to people that I was good with financial analysis because, again, there was this perception that women were not as good at modelling or were not as confident when working with numbers as they were potentially with qualitative work of writing proposals or working on presentations. This was factually accurate in my case, by the way, because I actually wasn't as competent in working on a model as I was in working on a PowerPoint, but that was more of a will problem than a skill problem. We'll talk a little bit about the skill versus will matrix at a later stage.

I needed someone to help me deal with the optics of that, not the reality of that. I didn't need extra help when building models. I needed extra help on what I needed to do to give the managers, leaders on my team the impression, the correct impression that I am competent at doing this thing, regardless of where I am relevant to my other skills.

Liking Sponsors Is Optional

The thing I should also point out is that the person whom I asked to mentor me on this topic and provide some coaching was not someone I liked. I respected them and what they had achieved in their career, but I certainly believed that they'd gone about it in a way that I felt did not align with my personal value system and my belief in a collaboration community over competition. They had something really important that they could teach me, so I got the lesson I could get from them, the thing that I wanted to understand from them, and then I left that relationship. Again, they weren't doing it out of the goodness of their heart. There were certainly advantages that they got from fulfilling their responsibility as a partner, providing someone else with support, mentorship, and eventually sponsorship. It was one of those situations where I realised that we actually have to like our coach or our mentor. Our coach shouldn't be telling us anything really about themselves if they're doing strict appreciative inquiry coaching. Coaches are trying to get us towards a goal, so they really don't need to give us very much information about themselves, nor do they need to be experts in anything we're doing to be able to help you. All they need to do is be good at asking the right questions and asking them in ways that really stimulate our thinking and ability to solve our challenges.

Similarly, sponsors, while they're putting their names on the line for you, we don't have to *like* them for doing that. I would not suggest that we work with people whom we actively dislike or have serious moral issues with, but if it's someone we just don't personally click with, it's perfectly fine to have them as our sponsor. As long as both of us understand the nature of our relationship, exactly what each of us is getting out of that relationship and what we need to give in return, it's possible.

I think the only situation where not liking the person who is supporting us is problematic is in the case of a mentor, because mentors provide us with information about how they have personally approached things. They're giving us advice based on their personal approach to examining certain challenges or reasoning through them. If we do not respect and like that person, it's going to be really difficult for us to trust in their guidance and implement it accordingly. So, while we don't have to like our coaches and sponsors, we should definitely try to, as well as our mentors, at least to some degree.

Incidentally, when I want someone to be my sponsor, I don't ask them to be a sponsor. I prefer a soft launch for these relationships and instead ask them to be my mentor. It's a longer process, but it gives us time to see if their values align with yours. Do they have insights we respect? Are they genuinely supportive, or are they just posturing? Once we've established a rapport and feel confident in their influence, we can shift the dynamic toward sponsorship.

Of course, not every relationship starts smoothly. Sometimes, you'll need to turn a hater into a sponsor. Sometimes the only thing we can do to neutralise someone less than supportive or even actively unkind is to link our success to their success. It is very difficult to criticise someone who is getting career advice from you publicly. I have done this a few times, even though I had zero interest in the actual advice they offered. I started my efforts to woo them small. I appealed to their ego and found ways to build a bridge with mutual interests or connections. It's like working with a skittish child or a very guarded colleague. We don't patronise them, but we do have to make it clear that their criticism has made us think that they have things to teach us.

I was always surprised by how much I accidentally learned from these former critics once they switched to Team Bontle. What I didn't know then was that a critic's self-esteem may be more fragile than it should be when they have had so much success. They want to be helpful to others and feel like they don't get to do that enough. Asking for their advice gave them the opportunity to be nicer people without having to acknowledge their initially unhelpful behaviour.

Another thing that should be obvious at this point is that a sponsor is never a peer. Our peers might be wonderful colleagues and friends, but they don't have the clout to elevate you. Sponsors in completely different industries or functions are probably also somewhat useless. I fully appreciate that it is way more intimidating to put ourselves out there than with a leader several layers above us, but it is what it is. We need someone higher up, ideally as high as possible. If we're already senior, that might mean targeting the CEO or even someone influential in our industry outside our organisation.

Sponsorship is about more than just having someone cheer us on. It's also about seizing the opportunities they create for you. Those opportunities? They're not always going to feel great. They'll be stretch assignments—things we're not entirely sure we can do. That's the point. Growth happens in discomfort. Lean into it.

TRY THIS: WHO HAS YOUR BACK?

Map your professional networks or relationships into one of the following buckets:

- **Mentor**: *Who provides advice based on experience?*

- **Coach**: *Who helps you find your own answers?*

- **Sponsor**: *Who actively advocates for you?*

- **Ally**: *Who supports you but lacks sponsor influence?*

Where are you strongest? Where are you weakest? What relationship gaps do you need to fill? Identify one key relationship to develop in the next quarter, with specific actions to strengthen it.

Part V
Now What?

Chapter 15

Corporate Is A Cult. You Can Be One Too!

P ropaganda can become one of your best friends.

It sounds unhinged right now, but trust me, we want to be a cult. That isn't a typo. I did not say 'join the cult.' I really did say 'be the cult.'

It is not a choice we will make lightly, but if we want to make it into plus 6-figure salaries executive roles, we better lean into the Cult of We pretty quickly.

Let's zoom out a little. As the whole first chunk of this book discussed, there are so many places where NDs feel alienated, isolated, ignored, or otherwise mistreated. There are so many norms that apply in the corporate world that do not benefit NDs in any way; many of these erode the self-belief that NDs have in themselves. We are told to bring our whole selves to work and, in so doing, destroy our whole selves when others reject them. We are told to be assertive and clear in what we want, but when we dare to speak up, we're told that we should know our place and stay in our lane.

We are meant to believe that our work will speak for itself, that if we collect the right favour from the right people, we will somehow find the ability to proceed and progress in the organisation. But the truth is that the company that we're in is trying to recruit us as members of its cult. It wants us to assimilate with the way that it believes it values its leaders. It wants us to continue to obey what it needs unquestioningly and, in fact, trust that the leaders understand the bigger picture or strategy that we couldn't possibly wrap our minds around, that it is supposed to benefit everyone in the cult and its beliefs. But the reality is that cult leaders benefit themselves. They may not even fully believe in the ideas of the cult in the worst, most cynical cases. Still, it is in their self-interest to continue to sustain the illusion that the cult is doing good work and that the possibilities of reward in this cult are increased by doing exactly what the leader of this cult wants.

It is really difficult not to get pulled into the cult of corporate simply by virtue of need. We have to feed ourselves and potentially others. We need clothes, shelter, all of those other things, which, unfortunately, require money. So, as much as people might say that we can always leave a toxic employer or choose ourselves, set our boundaries, blah, blah... the reality is that we may not be in a situation where we can leave that environment. We may be dependent on that environment, at least in the short term, for a variety of reasons that we should not feel bad or despondent about. Instead, we should recognise that it is very hard to groom someone twice. It is a terrible way to think about engaging with others. I certainly would never suggest that anyone groom anyone, but corporations are not people.

They are a collection of people, but somehow, in that collection, we lose a sense of individual responsibility and individual culpability such that our behaviour becomes 'okay' when we're in a corporation and representing the corporation in a way that it absolutely would not be if we were just us with no company backing. Now, the challenge of this, of course, is that the corporation is its own cult leader; it has no problem grooming us for its cause. It starts slowly with rewards and wooing in the recruitment process. It works really hard to create an amazing experience and impression from the outside of what joining this cult will look like. It may spend years grooming us in ways that we don't even understand through branding, marketing, reputation, and all sorts of trigger levers that are designed to pull on our psychological weaknesses, strengths, biases, and patterns to get us to engage in buying into this cult.

How do we avoid this? Easy. We need to have indoctrinated and groomed ourselves into the Cult of You. We can't be members of two cults, so we need to embrace the Cult of You to the extent that we are no longer capable of being pulled into another cult.

My high school history teacher made a solid effort at trying to groom me. I did not understand the level of attention that he was paying me, the strange comparisons with his wife that he was making, or the need to isolate me and pull me away from my friends. All of these things indicated a desire by this man to groom me for his purposes. Luckily, I never found out what those purposes were because he was too late. I had already been indoctrinated by someone else.

My father had groomed me, not for sexual purposes but certainly for his own entertainment, his plans, his greed, his ego, and his own need to be self-fulfilled through my identity and achievements. There was a plus side to his utterly unhinged 'make Bontle into a white dude CEO' thought experiment that I referenced earlier: his brainwashing had already taken hold so thoroughly that I was unavailable to be groomed by anyone else for anything else. While I certainly would have preferred not to have experienced that late-stage capitalist flavour of child abuse, the experience has subsequently served me very well in all contexts where people really wanted to convince me that their cult was the best. Until I'd had a lot of therapy and a lot of healing, I was still very firmly in the cult of my father. His way was the only way, not out of love or belief in his system but out of fear and concern for the consequences. Once I was an adult and able to have some distance and independence from my father, that was something I overcame. Still, those lessons will never truly be unlearned. The thing about trauma is that we keep returning to it and repeating the patterns it trapped us in. We go back to what we know because that is what is normal to you. I found myself repeatedly returning to spaces that wanted me to join their cult.

I've been very lucky not to replicate the abuse patterns of my childhood in my personal life. But, in my professional life, I cannot deny that I tend to find these charismatic leaders who want me to think and behave in a certain way, who are very happy to leap praise and adoration on me if it means that I am more willing to believe what they tell me and my role in achieving their desires. I joined my university's debating society, an incestuous misogynist group of young adults far too smart to have the kind of social skills required to interact without some level of condescension or derision. I got so into that cult that I married a fellow member. I joined a massive, very well-known consulting company. Over a decade since I first joined, I still refer to that company and its employees as 'we', not 'them'. There are a lot of jokes about how cultish top-tier consulting is. I knew the jokes, laughed alone, but completely dove into it anyway. That job gave me the career I have today. I knew it even when I was still in it. Had it not been for a certain very public scandal that necessitated a one-year sabbatical in investment banking, I would never have been so ungrateful and so duplicitous as to leave the cult. I had no desire to be rescued.

This brainwashing had its advantages. It was particularly helpful to get me through the worst of working 16 or 18-hour days for weeks or months on end, or to deal with the toxicity of partners who have only each other to hold them accountable, no higher oversight or disciplinary bodies than that. To keep revenues flowing, they needed young people to sacrifice their bodies in the same way as miners or sex workers, wholeheartedly without concern for their safety, simply by the necessity of getting the job done. The cult requires people to put aside their family, their health, their aspirations, and sometimes their value systems in order to do what's right for the cult. Most importantly, we may never forget that our success will only be possible with the success of the cult; we can never make it without them.

Now, all of that is incredibly toxic and quite depressing. It is reality, though. It is the way that most corporations are set up and how they engage with their employees, whether they're willing to recognise that or not. The helpful thing to think about here is that we cannot be a member of two cults at the same time. If we do not wish to be groomed, abused, or manipulated by the corporations or organisations we're in, we become our own cult. If we are a cult, we can have that level of unwavering support and adoration, which means we are willing to do almost anything to advance the mission, beliefs, and well-being of the cult.

Like I said at the start of this chapter, we are a cult. We are not the kind of cult that requires multiple members or demands people destroy their lives in reverence of its leader. We are, however, the kind of cult that is fanatical in its support of its ideals, its values, and its way of life. We are the kind of cult where we wholeheartedly believe our cult will succeed as long as we pour enough belief and determination into ignoring what anyone else is trying to tell us about the cult.

This cult is the type where positive illusions about the cult are important to sustain our support for the cult. We can question the cult to some degree. We can try to understand the origins of the cult's beliefs and values, but at the end of the day, we are encouraged to accept them as truth. We can question behind closed doors, but in public, we will always back it, even when no one else will. If we do not treat our career and ourselves like we are a cult, it's very easy to be side-tracked. It's very easy to be distracted. It's very easy to be brainwashed by others into believing that we are nowhere near as good as we are, and let a past version of us make decisions for a future you.

Put the person we want to be ahead of the person we currently are. Imagine ourselves as someone who has already achieved greatness, who has already achieved their goals, for whom time is simply the price that is paid for achieving that greatness. All of that would have a fundamentally good impact on how we see ourselves in a corporate sense.

Incidentally, I would never recommend that we adopt the idea of the cult of we in our personal lives for many reasons. Still, the principal among them is that relationships, interpersonal relations, communities, families, and friendship groups can't be cults if they are authentic and healthy. What they want is for us to be happy, productive people, re-gardless of what they get out of us. Acting as though our beliefs, our way of doing things, and our values supersede those of anyone else is an unhinged way to lead our personal life and certainly the recipe for unhappiness. Again, it returns to the intention of cult membership. People join a cult because they're trying to find a safe harbour in the storm of uncertainty, ambiguity, general confusion, and sadness in the world. Our life should be that safe harbour—everyone we love should be there with you. A cult of one in every aspect of our life is a terrible idea. We are a function of the people we know, love, and hang out with. Hold onto those connections.

One of the things which I often use as both a motivator and comforter is to remember that whatever I do or don't do at the office doesn't matter to the people who love me. No mistake will make them stop loving me. I will not stop loving them as a result of doing any part of my job. Sometimes, we're kind of a trash friend. Still, our best friends are always going to embrace us, hopefully, call us out and get us to get our stuff together. They won't abandon us for being who we are, even if, at that moment, that person is a little bit of trash.

Corporations are never going to behave the same way. There are no free passes for being bad at our job because we're going through some stuff. So, the 'cult of you' is something that should apply only in our professional life and only because we need to groom ourselves before anybody else grooms us.

This book, therefore, is about trying to build the 'cult of you', understanding what values and beliefs we are striving for, and understanding how to indoctrinate ourselves (create affirmations and manifestations that will serve us rather than break you). It's about how to deal with criticism from (often neurotypical) outsiders and not letting that judgment or criticism sway us in our belief in the cult of we or belief in succeeding at whatever our outcomes and desires may be. As in all cults, stay entirely focused on you. What other cults or cult leaders are doing, what other people or employees are doing, and whether our peers are absolutely smashing it or falling dismally behind we is irrelevant. Their behaviours, achievements, or failures have zero impact on our cult and its ability to be successful.

Everything that makes the cult succeed is from within the cult, not from without the cult. The cult does not seek to bring in outsiders as allies, supporters, or even affiliates. You're either in or we're out. If we're out, they don't care about you, as long as we do not do anything to interfere with, dissuade, or pull away their members. They do not compare their success as a cult to other cults. They're only trying to build something strong. Something resilient as far as their own membership base and their own identity. They very rightly understand that the success or failure of other cults has no bearing on their ability to succeed or fail.

Similarly, whatever other people are doing, how they choose to behave in the workplace, or what their values and principles have nothing to do with you, so forget them.

Our cultish self-belief will be required to make it to the most senior levels of corporate organisations, so embrace delusion.

We have this weird idea that if people do not want to be senior managers or executives, there's something wrong with them or that they are failing in some way in their duty to be successful in society. This is absolutely not the case.

Some people believe that feminism, for example, is set back by women who choose to be caregivers or choose to be subservient to men. Honestly, that kind of BS was invented by the patriarchy to make us hate and fight against each other. The more that we can fight against each other, the more divided we are, and the easier we are to indoctrinate and be tricked into believing in the cult of patriarchy. That's a cult that they've been trying to groom us into for years, regardless of our gender. Some of us are still members, trying to get out of it. It isn't easy to opt out of it entirely because it's everywhere: from the way the governments try to control what we do with our bodies all the way down to how we see ourselves in the mirror and what we believe is required of us to be attractive to others in many cases, to men specifically.

The same goes for ADHD employees. Wanting to go in, do the minimum, finish exactly on time, and not spare our work a single thought after our laptop is closed is totally chill. We don't need to be a poster child for what is possible when we embrace neurodiversity in the workplace. Absolutely do not drink that Kool-Aid.

If we can groom and co-opt ourselves, our peace of mind will be much safer from the indoctrination of capitalism, the patriarchy, and ableism. Start our own cult or risk becoming a member of someone else's.

TRY THIS: EMBRACE THE CULT OF YOU

If you are going to be a cult and you are working on a personal brand anyway, don't stop halfway. Fully commit to the bit!

1. What's your logo? Have you got a tagline?

2. What are your values? Any mantras you need to be repeating every morning?

3. Who are you trying to recruit to your team?

4. How are you going to get more followers?

And, most importantly, how are you going to look after The Boss (i.e., you)? They're called 'cults of personality' for the reason. Embrace making yourself the centre of something in a way your therapist will (probably) be cool with.

Chapter 16

The Last Lie: If It Hasn't Happened Yet, It's Not Going to Happen

J ust because your big break hasn't happened yet doesn't mean you're a failure. Success does not have an expiry date.

This is another example of beliefs that do not serve us. Believing that we should have done more by now, that everyone is ahead of us, that we peaked in high school, or that we are falling behind others, are all ingredients of a self-doubt soup with some extra RSA sprinkled in there because why not. Another one I hate: The lie that all of us are equally able to 'get ahead' if we just work hard enough only serves those who thrive based on other people's hard work. Much of the rhetoric around this notion of equality promotes a toxic, often masculine, work culture that discourages helping others and condemns anyone who doesn't 'succeed' as simply lacking willpower or desire. It assumes that everyone has equal opportunities, talents, and mindsets to achieve their goals, ignoring systemic inequalities. This unrealistic ideal suggests that people are solely responsible for their inputs and outcomes, disregarding the many unfair advantages that shape people's lives from birth.

For instance, those who typically promote this 'we all had the same starting point' narrative are often from financially secure backgrounds with white-collar professions and few opportunities to experience systemic oppression for themselves. The advantages of such a starting point compound from early childhood, depending on factors like access to nutrition, geographical location, and family wealth. For some, the 'geographical lottery' means growing up in a prosperous country; for others, it means facing daily survival challenges. Even when children are born into the same community, outcomes vary due to factors like parental support, emotional resources, and early childhood development opportunities, which are often limited by lack of access.

The same pattern occurs in sports, where children deemed 'talented' are placed in top teams, receiving better coaching resources. This divide compounds over time, even though a child in the 'C' team may have the same talent as one in the 'A' team. Privileged children have the support and resources that amplify their abilities. Without this support, talent alone often cannot compensate; children in lower teams face additional hurdles to improving.

This momentum continues into adult life, often unnoticed by the privileged. From being streamed into the 'smart' class, to getting allocated to the residence with the university's top students, there is a snowball effect. Going to a great university meant I was introduced to the Firm early, and working there uplevelled what was possible even years after I left.

These compounded privileges mean that I don't have the same 24 hours as others, and I haven't for 15 years. For example, a woman with a similar background to mine but working a blue-collar job may have to wake up early, prepare meals, commute for hours, spend her day labouring without seeing her children, and only return home to more household work. This life is not a choice; it's a situation created by limited opportunities and systemic barriers. For such a woman, personal development or self-care might be an hour of stolen time—an indulgence rather than a necessity. Meanwhile, I work a white-collar job with flexible hours, leaving me ample time in the evening to focus on personal development, self-care, or additional work. I work out four times a week and engage in artistic activities a few times a month. These unfair advantages compound over time; even how I age will differ because of my privileges.

This is why it's irrational to expect everyone to achieve equally. We invalidate the efforts of those who work incredibly hard without similar starts. For most people, there isn't a true 24 hours available between work, sleep, commutes, family obligations, and basic self-care. The reality is that these responsibilities keep them locked in a cycle with little time for personal advancement, while I have the luxury of hours each day for self-improvement.

My starting position was vastly different from someone else's, which is why I never encourage people to compare themselves to me or anyone else. Privilege shapes those hours, compounding opportunities in ways that make the idea of equal time an illusion.

David Neeleman was 39 years old when he founded JetBlue Airways in 1999. Mel Robbins was 42 when her '5 Second Rule' TED Talk changed her life. Sir James Dyson was living off his wife's teacher's salary and had made 5,126 failures before he developed the first working prototype of a bagless vacuum cleaner at 49 years old (Salter, 2007). You don't need a 'best before' label. You can always be fresh.

Regardless of what happened in the past, don't allow a past version of you to make decisions for a future version of you.

You might worry that your ADHD symptoms, like interrupting others when excited, losing track of conversations, or being inconsistent in your focus, will undermine your credibility as a potential manager. That may be a fair concern, but we can't change our brains. That implies that our only option is to hide our ADHD traits. Even with our typically squiggly careers, the journey to leadership is less fun when you spend most of it in hiding.

What I have learned is that trying to mask these traits consumes valuable mental energy that we could be using to lead effectively. The organisations that benefit most from ADHD leadership are those that appreciate our strengths: our creativity, our ability to hyperfocus on important problems, our outside-the-box thinking, and our genuine passion for what we do.

When up show up authentically, challenge your limiting beliefs with evidence, and recognise the complex interplay of diversity in all its forms, you become a more effective leader. You create spaces where others can bring their authentic selves too, which leads to more innovative, inclusive, and successful teams.

So, the next time you are in that boardroom or strategy meeting feeling hesitant to speak up, remember: your unique perspective is valuable precisely because it is different. Lower your standards for what counts as a 'saying something smart' contribution,' ignore the negative stories you tell yourself, and create the scaffolding that you need to be successful.

Like I said: success does not have an expiry date. It's only too late if you never start.

References

1. Arnst, C. (2003) cited in Patton, E. (2009) 'When diagnosis does not always mean disability: The challenge of employees with Attention Deficit Hyperactivity Disorder (ADHD)', Journal of Workplace Behavioral Health, 24(3), pp. 326-343.

2. CIPD (2024) Neuroinclusion at Work Report 2024. Available at: https://www.cipd.org/globalassets/media/knowledge/knowledge-hub/reports/2024-pdfs/2024-neuroinclusion-at-work-report-8545.pdf (Accessed: 31 December 2024).

3. Cleveland Clinic. (2024). Neurotransmitters. Available at: https://my.clevelandclinic.org/health/articles/22513-neurotransmitters (Accessed: 23 May 2025).

4. Faraone, S. V., Banaschewski, T., Coghill, D., Zheng, Y., Biederman, J., Bellgrove, M. A., Newcorn, J. H., Gignac, M., Al Saud, N. M., Manor, I., Rohde, L. A., Yang, L., Cortese, S., Almagor, D., Stein, M. A., Albatti, T. H., Aljoudi, H. F., Alqahtani, M. M. J., Asherson, P., ... & Wang, Y. (2021). The World Federation of ADHD International Consensus Statement: 208 Evidence-based Conclusions about the Disorder. Neuroscience & Biobehavioral Reviews, 128, 789–818. https://doi.org/10.1016/j.neubiorev.2021.01.022

5. Garber, P. (2001) 'Employment of adults with learning disabilities and ADHD: Reasons for success and implications for resilience', ADHD Report, 9(4), pp. 1-5.

6. Hallowell, E.M. & Ratey, J.J. (2021) ADHD 2.0: New Science and Essential Strategies for Thriving with Distraction—from Childhood through Adulthood. New York: Ballantine Books.

7. Hotte-Meunier, A., Sarraf, L., Bougeard, A., Bernier, F., Voyer, C., Deng, J., El Asmar, S., Stamate, A. N., Corbière, M., & Villotti, P. (2024). Strengths and challenges to embrace attention-deficit/hyperactivity disorder in employment—A systematic review. Neurodiversity, 2(1), 1–13. https://doi.org/10.1177/27546330241287655

8. Jackson, B., & Farrugia, D. (1997). Diagnosis and treatment of adults with attention deficit hyperactivity disorder. Journal of Counseling & Development, 75(4), 312–319. https://doi.org/10.1002/j.1556-6676.1997.tb02346.x

9. Matza, L. S., Paramore, C., & Prasad, M. (2005). A review of the economic burden of ADHD. Cost effectiveness and resource allocation : C/E, 3, 5. https://doi.org/10.1186/1478-7547-3-5

10. Nadeau K. G. (2005). Career choices and workplace challenges for individuals with ADHD. Journal of Clinical Psychology, 61(5), 549–563. https://doi.org/10.1002/jclp.20119

11. Neilsen, J. (2024) '24 ADHD Statistics and Facts for 2024', ADHDAdvisor.org, 15 February. Available at: https://www.adhdadvisor.org/learn/adhd-statistics-and-facts (Accessed: 11 May 2025)

12. Norman, S. (2023) Workplace ADHD Statistics in the UK. Available at: https://augmentive.io/blog/workplace-adhd-statistics-uk (Accessed: 23 May 2025).

13. Patton, E. (2009). When diagnosis does not always mean disability: The challenge of employees with Attention Deficit Hyperactivity Disorder (ADHD). Journal of Workplace Behavioral Health, 24(3), 326–343. https://doi.org/10.1080/15555240903176161

14. Pistoia, J.C. (2023) ADHD and Disrespectful Behavior. Available at: https://psychcentral.com/adhd/adhd-and-disrespectful-behavior (Accessed: 23 May 2025).

15. Robbins, R. (2017). The untapped potential of the ADHD employee in the workplace. Cogent Business & Management, 4(1), Article 1271384. https://doi.org/10.1080/23311975.2016.1271384Salter, C. (2007) 'Failure doesn't suck', Fast Company. Available at: https://www.fastcompany.com/59549/failure-doesnt-suck (Accessed: 4 January 2025).

16. Turjeman-Levi, Y., Itzchakov, G. and Engel-Yeger, B. (2024) 'Executive function deficits mediate the relationship between employees' ADHD and job burnout', AIMS Public Health, 11(1), pp. 294–314. doi: 10.3934/publichealth.2024015 (Accessed: 24 March 2025).

17. Weiss, M. D., & Weiss, J. R. (2004). A guide to the treatment of adults with ADHD. The Journal of clinical psychiatry, 65 Suppl 3, 27–37.

18. World Federation of ADHD (2021) 'The World Federation of ADHD International Consensus Statement: 208 Evidence-based conclusions about the disorder', Neuroscience & Biobehavioral Reviews, 128, pp. 789–818. Available at: https://doi.org/10.1016/j.neubiorev.2021.01.022 (Accessed: 24 March 2025).

Acknowledgements

This book was written very fast because I had the best team around me.

Thanks to the Wired Differently family for taking me in, especially Rhi, Elliot, and Polly, who have to deal with a lot of random WhatsApps.

The members of my squad who were more involved than others in the process of writing and editing this book: Zhe H, Busang S, Reabetswe M, Zulaika K, Richard C, Dara O, Gilda L, Jen van H, Lunel van Z, Corina R, Fiona M, Vimbayi K, Cleola K, and Farah M.

Thanks to the people who became test subjects for all my ideas in leadership in the last two years: Billy M, Alessandro, Nicole, Rohan, Zena, Charley, and Victoria.

I thank my beta readers, Sherelee Lockhart and Lebogang Maila, for their comments, questions, and corrections. A special thanks to Anthony Gribben-Lisle, who read this book more than once and provided the most helpful and detailed insights and advice. I am incredibly grateful to all three of you.

My work wife, Sara-Louise Ackrill, who helped me excavate my love of writing from the dumpster fire of 2021/22. I am so grateful for you.

Last and never least, my family: Caleb Philander, Patrick Ngondweni, Pat Senne (a mom with a twist), Busang Senne (my favourite sister and person on Earth), and Logan Senne (yes, I know she's a dog).

About the author

Bontle Senne is an interim transformation leader, keynote speaker, AuD-HD author, publisher, and coach. Her extraordinary career has included everything from leading billion-dollar megamergers in the UK to rebuilding a West African national education system for 1.2 million pupils and working with start-ups and SMEs on frugal innovation.

Bontle began her career in publishing as an intern at a feminist trade publisher and a writer of Young Adult literature, publishing six acclaimed novels in South Africa and Ghana. She was shortlisted for Africa's prestigious Golden Baobab Prize for children's literature in 2014.

The ADHD Boss is her eighth book.

www.ingramcontent.com/pod-product-compliance
Lightning Source LLC
Chambersburg PA
CBHW031854200326
41597CB00012B/403